GREEN & AWAKE

PHOTOGRAPHY
by NAZLI DEVELI

COPYRIGHT 2019
ALL RIGHTS RESERVED
by *NAZLI DEVELI*

Second Printing , 2020
ISBN 9781794481947
Published by Nazlı Develi via Amazon.com

For information about permission to reproduce selections
from this book, write to nazli@gurmevegan.com
www.gurmevegan.com
www.greenandawake.com

- CREATOR OF GURMEVEGAN·COM -

Nazli Develi

GREEN & AWAKE

GOURMET VEGAN COOKBOOK

WITH A PINCH OF NORDIC FLAVOUR

GREEN & AWAKE

CONTENT

GREEN & AWAKE

Author & Plant-Based Chef

Nazli Develi

ABOUT

Hi there. I am Nazlı, a plant based chef, raw pastry instructor, menu designer and cookbook author. I love to cook so much! I spent my childhood in the kitchen with my chef grandfather. After many corporate experiences and learning processes in my life journey, I had a deep spiritual experience in a pachamama ceremony. In 2014, when I questioned the abnormality of an animal-eating diet, was introduced to the concept of "Veganism" and I had a quick transition shortly after the awakening.

In this book, I combined the knowledge I have aquired for years with my intuitive side and tried perfecting art of plant-based cooking by experimenting my recipes .

In addition to designing menus for various hotels & restaurants around Nordics, I also share my ethusiasm through Instagram, cookbooks and my website gurmevegan.com. I invite you to find out positive effects of green & awake food on to the mental and physical impacts sizing the journey of your life.

This is my first cookbook that helps people become better dishes by using a minimalist approach to cooking. It allows me to use my food science knowledge for good. The amount of equipment, with easy steps involved, and the time we spend in the kitchen to a minimum so we can focus what's important. It's about simple gourmet food that is easy to prepare and still fun and satisfying to eat.

enjoy and thanks

GREEN & AWAKE

Green represents food from the nature,
Awake represents our inner awareness.

MINIMAL INGREDIENTS

This is related to time but I wanted to spell it out separately. I'm always looking to minimalise the number of steps needed in a recipe. I strive to keep the instructions concise but easy to follow.

MINIMAL EQUIPMENT

I've never been a fan of single-use kitchen equipment and I know that like me, most people are cooking in pretty basic kitchens. This book may be quicker, easier to prepare with a food processor.

I see sharing and spreading experiences as a social responsibility towards future generations.

When we look into the world, insatiable ego, ambition, endless wars, persecution of other creatures are always due to negative energy.

The person who eats the body of a dead animal is fed with the negative energy of the animal that is created by it's artificial and involuntary farm life.

A person spreads this negative energy to the others and it leads to a life that has been in vain with the bad karma that it creates.

On the way to individual improvement, to nourish vegan is imperative. Vegan nourishing also encircles other spiritual sides of the foods such as foods having a higher vibration which are healthier rather than the dead ingredients.

Also there is more about the spiritual side; thoughts of the person who makes the meal, affects the quality of the food. Being in touch with natural - not fabricated - ingredients during the cooking process, feeling the nature and it's enormous offerings, makes people happier than unnatural ingredients.

In this book, I have prepared gourmet recipes that you will enjoy more and more when you stop eating animals.

FOR THOSE WHO ARE INTERESTED IN MORE...

The state of your mind while you are cooking, directly affects the quality of food. It is possible to transform every meal into a medical joy by conscious cooking.

Each color, sound, thought and emotion have its own vibration. We're all made of vibrational energy and connected spiritually by the energy. We need to consume the energy in various forms such as water, air and food.

All connected

We do not need only vitamins or minerals. It is the aura of the food and what kind of spirit joins when it is brought together. In short, while eating, we take our thoughts or the emotions and thoughts of others.

APPE-TIZERS

NOTHING IS BETTER THAN A BITE-SIZED APPETIZER TO START OFF A MEAL.

Whether you're hosting cocktail hour, celebrating with friends, or watching the big game, you'll need an appetizer. You will find the best of tasty appetizers with full photos and tips on how to make them in this chapter.

CHEESE

FERMENTED MACADAMIA

Nuts contain levels of phytic acid equal to or higher than those of grains. Therefore those consuming nut butters or nut flours, will take in phytate levels similar to those in unsoaked grains...

When we ferment the nuts, phytates are eliminated. Fermentation of every kind makes foods more digestible. If you are particularly careful with phytate consumption, you can soak your nuts or seeds first and then make nut cheese with them, doubly predigesting them. I recommend this step. It is so easy to do an overnight soak on nuts. And when you rinse away their dirty water, it is heartening to know how much good you've already done, even before taking the next step in fermentation. So cutting down on phytates every time we eat means that we get more minerals out of our food, instead of them being bound and unattainable by our bodies.

Another benefit of fermented nut cheeses is that fermenting makes nutrients more bio-available. So the nuts, herbs, spices, garlic, coconut oil, anything you add will be more powerful nutritionally than it would be otherwise.

MACADAMIA CHEESE

INGREDIENTS

Raw macadamia nuts	220 GR
Acidophilus Probiotic	4 GR
Filtered Water	1/3 CUP
Nutritional Yeast	2 TBSP
Lemon Juice	2 TBSP
Sea Salt	1/4 TABLESPOON
Fresh Dill	1/2 BUNCH
Garlic	

METHOD
RAW

TIME
50 MINUTE

SERVING
6 PERSON

DIFFICULTY
10/7

PLACE NUTS IN A JAR. COVER WITH FILTERED WARM WATER AND CLOSE THE JAR. LET IT REST IN THE ROOM AT LEAST 1 HOUR. THEN PLACE IN THE FRIDGE FOR 6 HOURS. THIS PROCESS WILL ACTIVATE THE NUTS AND ALSO YIELDS A NEUTRAL NUT FLAVOR.

Set 6 tablespoons water nuts aside. Strain and rise nuts. Place nuts and 6 tablespoons water into the food processor. Mix on high speed until silky smooth. If you are using probiotic powder then dissolve it in a little water. Then transfer into the food processor. Mix well. Transfer nut mixture into a nut milk bag. Gather up the ends to create a ball. Wrap the ends and squeeze out any excess moisture.

Place cheese in the dehydrator at 30 degrees for about 20-24 hours to let it ferment.

House with an average temperature of 25-30°C for 24 hours.

DIRECTIONS

STEP I

Once the fermentation time is up, open the cheesecloth and observe your nut cheese very carefully. You will probably notice that a yellowish crust has formed on top. That is totally normal. The inside of the nut cheese should be spongy. If there is pink or bluish spots, it indicates the presence of mold; throw away the cheese and restart. If everything is ok, transfer cheese from its cloth to a bowl and stir in nutritional yeast, garlic, lemon juice and salt.

STEP II

At this point you could add in other flavors whatever you like. If you like a stronger cheese flavor, add a bit more nutritional yeast. Form a log or ball on a piece of parchment paper and place in the fridge for overnight.

STEP III

Last step is rolling in a salty herby mixture. On a flat surface, spread out fresh dill or your herbs and sprinkle on some salt. Take your cheese and give it a good roll in the herbs. Place in the fridge at least 3 days to age the your cheese. If you like a softer cheese, you can use cashews instead of macadamia nuts, or a mix of both nuts. In that case, you will need less than ½ cup of water, because cashews are creamier to blend.

Bon Appetit

CULTURED CHEDDAR

This cultured vegan cheddar cashew cream cheese is incredibly simple to make and packed with all the beloved tanginess of the "real" thing. It actually tastes better than most commercial recipes. It is also spreadable, so this means perfect to serve with sandwiches or as an appetizer.

HOW TO MAKE AQUAFABA?

Rinse the chickpeas, transfer them to a pot, and cover with fresh water. Let it stand overnight. In the morning, check the level of the soaking water: If the chickpeas aren't completely submerged, add just enough water to cover them. Once the beans are cooked, use a strainer or fine sieve to strain the aquafaba into a large liquid measuring cup, and let it cool.

THIS SIMPLE CHEESE RECIPE IS FAST AND FRESH

TIME	SERVING	DIFFICULTY
20 MINUTE	6 PERSON	10 / 5

Spreadable

WHAT IS REJUVELAC? It is a fermented beverage that is inexpensive, easy to make, refreshing to drink and FULL of wonderful nutrients for your body. A healthy probiotic, it also has vitamins B, K and E, proteins, and enzymes. It is beneficial to your digestive system, promoting a healthy intestinal environment. It is also a great starter for raw nut cheese!

INGREDIENTS

Raw Cashews soaked	200	GR
Aquafaba OR Rejuvelac	250	ML
Lemon Juice	1/2	
Apple Cider Vinegar	1	TSP
Tomato Paste	1	TBSP
Miso	1	TSP
Paprika	1	TSP
Smoke Liquid	1	TSP
Turmeric	1/2	TSP
Nutritional Yeast	2	TBSP

DIRECTIONS

Blend soaked cashews and aquafaba in a high speed blender until smooth.

Strain mixture to remove large particles. Then transfer mixture to your blender again. Add lemon juice, tomato paste, turmeric, paprika, nutritional yeast, miso and then pulse in the blender to combine them well. Add apple cider vinegar and smoke liquid and blend again until silky smooth. Taste and add salt as you need. If the mixture is very thick, you can add some water (about 50 ml) and mix well afterwards.

LET IT REST

Pour mixture into a glass jar. Refrigerate at least 3 hours before using.

Bon Appetit

CHEDDAR
CULTURED

HOW TO MAKE REJUVELAC

Ingredients:

1/2 cup unsprouted raw whole grains,

2 cup water

Method:

1. Wash and drain your grains, place into a glass jar. Cover with filtered water.

2. Let your jar sit at room temperature away from direct sunlight for 6 to 8 hours.

3. Then drain the water. Rinse the grains a couple times. Drain water again and cover the top of jar with a cheesecloth or very thinly kitchen towel.

4. Let the grains sit at room temperature until sprouted, it takes about 1 to 2 days. Keep the grains from drying out by rinsing and draining them 2 to 4 times a day.

5. When your grains have started to sprout, rinse them one more time and drain well.

6. Fill your jar with filtered fresh water again. Let it ferment for 2 to 3 days.

7. When mixture started to ferment, you will see bubbles in the water. And then the water will seem cloudy. This is totally normal. when the mixture reach up to this, it is ready.

8. Strain the liquid into a new jar and keep in the refrigerator. It is ready to use for cultured cheese.

9. If you need more liquid, add more water in the jar to create second batch. It takes 1-2 days. Repeat the process for this. Keep your liquid and use sprouted grains in your salad.

I am a bit of an italian food lover and always looking for ideas and techniques for crafting a true Italian style pizza.

THE ART OF PIZZA MAKING

A FEW THINGS FOR CRAFTING A PIZZA LIKE PRO

LET IT REST

Make your dough 4 days before you need it. The dough needs to be refrigerated for about 3 to 4 days before you start to work with it. It has a better flavor when it sets for awhile.

Why does the local pizzeria's pizza taste better than the stuff you make at home? It's likely because their oven is hotter than yours. you should be baking your pizzas as hot as your oven will go- generally in the 550°F range —but if you want to up your game even further, consider a higher heat approach like skillet-broiler method.

ADD YOUR TOPPINGS WISELY

It's a given that whether you're making a cooked sauce or simply using hand-crushed tomatoes straight out of the can, you should be using a good brand.

AS FOR OTHER TOPPINGS, THE URGE TO GO CRAZY WITH THEM CAN BE INTENSE, BUT THE BEST PIES KEEP THE TOPPINGS MINIMAL AND BALANCED. I TRY TO MINIMALISE, ASKING MYSELF AT EACH STEP WHETHER WHAT I'M ADDING IS COMPLEMENTING THE INGREDIENTS I ADDED BEFORE, AND WHETHER THEY ALL COME TOGETHER INTO A SYNERGISTIC WHOLE THAT IS GREATER THAN THE SUM OF ITS PARTS.

Buon Appetito.

It's possible to make restaurant-quality pizza at home!

COCKTAIL PIZZA

BEET, CAPERS, ONION

GREEN & AWAKE

SKILLET-BROILER METHOD

Forget preheating the oven: just use the skillet. A skillet-broiler not only cooks via hot air like the oven, but more importantly, it adds a significant amount of radiant heat to the mix, cooking the top of the pizza directly with electro-magnetic waves—a much more efficient means of heat transfer. The difference between a skillet-broiler method is all in the texture: crispy and chewy, rather than soggy and limp.

COOK IN OLIVE OIL

Your toppings will be more unctuous and rich-tasting.

FRESH HERBS

Simply tear herbs gently with your hands over the finished crust

BLOOD TEMPERATURE

Mix together flour, yeast, olive, and water at 96 degrees for a perfect crust.

ITALIAN CUISINE

ITALIAN FOOD

method

4-6 PERSON

INGREDIENTS

Fresh Yeast	45	GR
Olive Oil	3	TBSP
Sea Salt	2	TSP
Warm Water	1	CUP
Whole Wheat Flour	3	CUPS
Coconut Sugar	1	TBSP

TOPPINGS

Red Onion	1	MEDIUM
Cherry Tomatoes	1/2	CUP
Beetroot	1	SMALL
Shiitake Mushrooms	100	GR
Vegan Parmesan	100	GR
Pine Nuts	30	GR
Capers	1	TBSP
Lemon Juice	1	TBSP
Garlic	2	CLOVES
Ground Mustard	1	TSP
Fresh Rosemary Leaves	A HANDFUL	

ADD PURPLE PLUM AND GREEN PEPPERS TO GET
UNIQUE FLAVOUR!

STEP I Melt yeast in warm water, add olive oil, coconut sugar and salt. Mix together well. Then add the flour, mix until get an elastic dough. Place the kneaded dough in an oiled bowl, cover with a warm towel, and let it triple in size in a warm place.

STEP II After 1 hour, place it in the fridge and use after 3-4 days for best results or to use in the same day, knead dough with your hands for about 2-3 minutes. Divide 2 or 3 pieces. Roll them into a nice shape. Bake in a skillet.

STEP III Heat up a large skillet pan, add olive oil, ground mustard, salt, lemon juice, thinly sliced onions, mushrooms, beets, pine nuts and garlic, cook over medium-high heat until golden brown. Top on your crust.

SPREAD SHREDDED VEGAN CHEESE AND COOK FOR A MINUTE OR TWO.
DECORATE WITH FRESH ROSEMARY LEAVES AND CAPERS.

RAW KALE CRACKERS

Living food, because cooking foods destroys more than 90% of its nutrition-al value and natural enzymes that the body needs to digest the food. Enzymes are more important than any other active element as an aid to digestion and health.

TIME

8 HOURS

SERVING

6 PERSON

DIFFUCULTY

10 / 7

TZATZIKI

150 gr. Raw Cashews
200 ml Water
3 tbsp Lemon Juice
1 tsp Garlic Granule
1/2 Sea Salt
1/8 Black Pepper
60 gr. Cucumber without Juice
3 tbsp Fresh Dill
1 tbsp Beet Powder to make it pink

These raw crackers are full of fabulous flavor, loaded with nutrients, and live enzyme

INGREDIENTS

70 gr. kale chopped in the food processor (measured after ribs removed)

1 teaspoon garlic granule,

4-5 piece sun dried tomatoes (35 gr.)

1 tablespoon dried rosemary,

4 tablespoon ground flaxseeds,

100 ml water,

2 tablespoon sesame seeds,

3 tablespoon chia seeds,

1 tablespoon fresh lemon juice,

2 tablespoon extra virgin olive oil,

1 tablespoon sprouted pea flour (or buck-wheat flour)

1/2 teaspoon salt to taste

DIRECTIONS

In a small bowl add 100 ml water and chia seeds, let them rest for 10 minutes.

Add all remaning ingredients into the food processor and mix until get dough consistency.Then add chia mix, blend again. Remove dough from the food processor. Make a ball with your hands. Place the ball between two sheets of parchment and roll out with a rolling pill as thin as possible, without breaking any of the edges.

Put the rolled out dough on a baking sheet and use a pizza cutter to make scores in the crackers for later. Dehydrate in the food dehydrator at 42 C for about 8 hours and then flip. Bake another 2 hours or until crisp on both sides if you need. Serve with tzatziki sauce if desired. To make tzatziki, blend all ingredients expect cucumber. Then transfer in a bowl, add cucumbers, stir well. Serve with crackers.

gurme vegan

RAW
KALE CRACKERS

GREEN ALMOND

A S P A R A G U S   S A L S A

GREEN ALMOND ASPARAGUS SALSA

METHOD
RAW

TIME
20 MINS

SERVING
5-6

DIFFICULTY
10 / 3

Living food

Green almonds are often served with just a sprinkling of sea salt. You can use them in pastas, stews, and salads. Add them to a jam, or even turn them into a beverage. If you're feeling ambitious, try this creative and refreshing recipe.

DIRECTIONS

STEP I   In a mixing bowl, toss the chopped onions, asparagus, green almonds, pepper and a pinch of salt with the red wine vinegar. Set aside to macerate for at least 15 -20 minutes.

STEP II   Next, add the capers, parsley and thyme to the bowl with marinated green almonds. Slowly whisk in the olive oil. Add salt and pepper to taste. Enjoy!

INGREDIENTS

120 gr. green almonds thinly sliced
1/2 bunch baby asparagus sliced thinly
1 medium red onion thinly sliced
2 tbsp red wine vinegar
2 tbsp pickled capers
A pinch of salt and chili pepper to taste
1 tbsp olive oil (optional)
1/4 bunch fresh thyme chopped
1/4 bunch fresh parsley chopped (optional)

THIS SALSA IS GENIUS, AND SUCH A GOOD WAY TO ENJOY
ASPARAGUS AND GREEN ALMONDS IN SPRING

Bon Appetit

CHEESY POTATOES

The original Irish potato – the one grown so widely in Ireland before the infamous famine - has been identified and bred to be resistant to late blight disease. "Irish Lumper" is a slightly oblong, knobby waxy white potato.

White Irish potatoes are among the most widely-grown worldwide. The tubers hold their shape when boiled or turned into potato salad, and can be roasted, broiled or fried. However, white potatoes are a little too dense to mash very well without getting gluey.

A PERFECT WAY OF ENJOYING WEEKEND BREAKFAST

TIME
20 MINUTE

SERVING
4 PERSON

DIFFICULTY
10 / 4

Cheesy

Cheesy and delicious these Oven Baked Cheesy Irish Potatoes are quick, easy and are the absolute perfect side dish to any meal! You can make cheesy potatoes a number of ways by changing how you make them or what you use to make them.

INGREDIENTS

White Potatoes	375	GR
Filtered Water	1	CUP
Maple Syrup	1	TBSP
Onion Powder	1/2	TSP
Plant Based Milk	75	ML
Ground Coriander	1/2	TSP
Sea Salt	1	TSP
White Rice Flour	4	TBSP
Garlic Powder	1/2	TSP
Nutritional Yeast	1	TBSP

TOPPINGS

A pinch of chili flakes, black and white sesame seeds.

DIRECTIONS

Wash, peel and cut quarter potatoes.
Place in a deep pot, cover with water , bring to boil until soften.

———

Discard the rest of water. Let potatoes to cool for 10-15 min.
Place all ingredients into the food processor, mix on high speed until get smooth and sticky mixture.
Pre-heat oven to 180 degrees. Place parchment paper into the baking tray.
Scoop 2 tbsp dough pieces and place onto the parchment paper.

Top with chili flakes, black and white sesame. Bake for 35-40 minutes or keep your eye out and remove from the oven once the tops are golden.
Cool for a few minutes before serving.

Bon Appetit

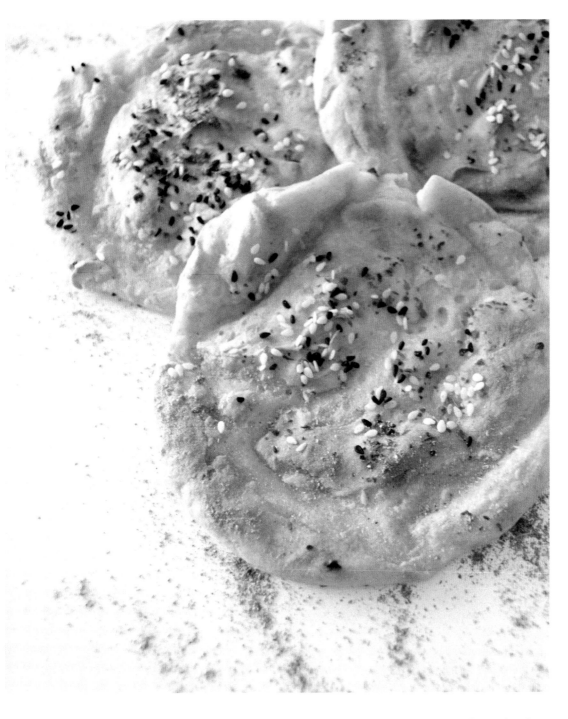

IRISH BONNIE

CHEESY POTATOES

Cheesy and delicious these Oven Baked Cheesy Irish Potatoes are quick, easy and are the absolute perfect side dish to any meal! You can make cheesy potatoes a number of ways by changing how you make them or what you use to make them.

FOCACCIA
BREAD

FOCACCIA

B R E A D

METHOD	**TIME**	**SERVING**	**DIFFUCULTY**
OVEN	2 HOUR	6-8	10 / 6

STEP I   In a large bowl, whisk together yeast, almond milk and 1 tbsp olive oil.
Pour flour in to the bowl. Mix together. Stir well with a wooden spoon. Cover bowl with a plastic wrap, let it rest for 30-35 minutes or until it begins to get bubbly.

STEP II   Knead dough with your hands, turn out on to a work surface. Knead well again. Place it into bowl , cover and let to rest it again for 10-15 minutes. Preheat oven to 50 degrees. Place bowl in to the oven for 40 minutes or until it has doubled in size.

STEP III   Remove bowl from the oven. Transfer it to a work surface. Knead and strech out with your hands. When the dough is smooth, coat it in a thin layer of 1 tbsp olive oil. Preheat oven to 220 degrees. Put a parchment paper in a pan. Flatten and shape the dough in a baking pan. Strech it into the corners.

STEP IV   Make deep holes with a teaspoon to put olives and tomatoes. Cut olives and tomatoes in two. Push them into the holes.
Drizzle a little bit extra olive oil if desired. Sprinkle sea salt and rosemary. Bake for 18-20 minutes or until golden browned. Remove from the oven, let it cool before serving.

I N G R E D I E N T S

Whole Wheat Flour	450	GR
Instant Yeast	10	GR
Unsweetned Almond Milk	300	ML
Sea Salt	1	TSP
Cherry Tomato	1	CUP
Olives	1/2	CUP
Olive Oil	1/2	CUP
Rosemary	2	TSP
Shallot	6-7	
Garlic Granule	2	TSP

THE SECRET TO THE BEST FOCACCIA BREAD IS GREAT TASTING OLIVE OIL. SINCE THERE IS QUITE A BIT USED, THE BREAD REALLY TAKES ON THE FLAVOR.

Bon Appetit

SPINACH CRACKERS

Did you know, you can make your own homemade crackers with just a couple of ingredients – and you can even make them green by adding spinach! These Spinach & Sesame Crackers are the perfect, vibrant and healthy snack! They are delicious to dip in hummus!

ROLL OUT THE DOUGH AS THIN AND AS EVEN AS POSSIBLE.

TIME	SERVING	DIFFICULTY
8 HOURS	6 PERSON	10 / 5

Chewy

A proper rolling pin helps a lot with rolling the dough evenly. It works best with a large rolling pin with rotating handles.

INGREDIENTS

Spinach Puree	400 GR
Onion Powder	1 TSP
Agave Syrup	1 TBSP
Garlic Powder	1/2 TSP
Salt	1 TSP
Lemon Juice	2 TBSP
Water	4 TBSP
Almond Meal or Sprouted Pea Flour	1 CUP
Flaxseed Meal	3 TBSP
Sauerkraut Seeds (optional)	3 TBSP
Sesame Seeds	2 TBSP

DIRECTIONS

In a small bowl add water and ground flax, let them rest for 10 minutes.

Add all remaning ingredients into the food processor and mix until get dough consistency.Then add flax mix, blend again. Remove dough from the food processor. Make a ball with your hands. Place the ball between two sheets of parchment and roll out with a rolling pill as thin as possible, without breaking any of the edges.

Put the rolled out dough on a baking sheet and use a pizza cutter to make scores in the crackers for later. Dehydrate for about 8 hours and then flip. Bake another 2 hours or until crisp on both sides if you need.

Bon Appetit

RAW

SPINACH CRACKERS

PORTOBELLO

MUSHROOMS FILLED SPINACH

PORTOBELLO MUSHROOMS

INGREDIENTS

Portobello Mushrooms	7 LARGE
Chopped Spinach	200 GR
Olive Oil	2 TBSP
Onion or Leek	1 MEDIUM
Soy Sauce or Tamari	2 TBSP
Vegan Parmesan	60 GR
Red Pepper Chopped	2 MEDIUM
Microgreens	2 TBSP
Sea Salt	1 TSP

METHOD	TIME	SERVING	DIFFUCULTY
OVEN	30 MINUTE	6 PERSON	10/3

PREP

WASH AND DRAIN MUSHROOMS, SET ASIDE ONE CAP TO SAUTE , SPRAY REMAINING 6 CAPS WITH OLIVE OIL COOKING SPRAY ON BOTH SIDES. PREHEAT OVEN TO 200 DEGREES.

Wash your veggies and drain. Chop onion or leek, cut the cap you set aside before , into small pieces. Chop red pepper.

Shred vegan parmesan very thinly. Place in medium bowl, set aside.

Portobello mushrooms have a robust meaty texture making them good for roasting, baking and stuffing.

DIRECTIONS

STEP I

Line a parchment paper in a baking tray. Place mushrooms onto the pan. Bake for 15 minutes or until turn golden brown. In a large pan, saute leek and peppers together in olive oil.

STEP II

Add chopped mushrooms, soy sauce and spinach. Cook on medium heat for about 4-5 minutes. Add salt and black pepper, stir and remove from the oven.

STEP III

Using a small spoon, fill your mushrooms with spinach mixture. Spread shredded vegan parmesan over the mushrooms. Bake for 10 minutes in the oven.. Decorate with microgreens, serve!

Bon Appetit

CHRUNCY EGGPLANTS

OVEN   50 MINS   2-3 PERSON   10/2

Designed for people who don´t like eggplants!

These bites are spicy, salty, savory and crispy. Guaranteed your satis-faction.

INGREDIENTS

Eggplants	3	MEDIUM
All dried bread powder	1	CUP
Ground flaxseed	2	TBSP
Water	5	TBSP
Sea Salt	1	TSP
Olive Oil	1	TBSP
Black Pepper	1/4	TSP
Red Pepper	1	TSP

STEP I Pre-heat oven to 200C. Cut eggplants 3/8" thick. Place them in a bowl, cover with water and let them rest for about 1 hours in order to remove their bitterness. Strain and dry your eggplant slices. Place them onto the parchment paper.

STEP II In a small bowl, mix flax seed and water. Let it rest in the fridge for 10 minutes. In a medium bowl place dried bread powder. Mix until combined well.

Take an eggplant slice. Dip it in the flax seed liquid. Then dip it in the dried bread powder flour so it is coated, shake off excess. Then place it on the baking sheet again. Drizzle with olive oil. Sprinkle salt and peppers. Repeat process for all. Bake your eggplants in the oven for 50 minutes turning the half way through until golden browned.

FOR BEST RESULT, SERVE WARM!

This recipe goes well with any main dish.

W I T H   A R R A B B I A T A

HOW TO MAKE SAUCE?

Place all sauce ingredients into the food processor mix on high speed until completely smooth.
Pour mixture into the sauce pan, cook on medium heat for 3-4 minutes. Place it into a small sauce bowl.

INGREDIENTS

1 small onion chopped,
2 large tomatoes,
1 tablespoon tomato paste,
1 teaspoon garlic powder

1 teaspoon oregano,
1 teaspoon red chili pepper,
1 teaspoon sea salt,
2 tablespoon olive oil

1 medium carrot chopped,
6-7 olive,
7-8 large fresh basil leaves,
1/8 teaspoon blackpepper

SERVE WARM WITH CHRUNCY EGGPLANTS

BROAD BEANS

S O U P

METHOD
RAW

TIME
10 MINS

SERVING
2-3

DIFFICULTY
10 / 2

DIRECTIONS

1. Clean and cut onion, garlic and carrots. Place in a large pot. Cook with a little olive oil until soften. Then add vegetable stock.

2. Clean artichoke leaves till you reach the heart. Then cut in half vertical, clean fuzzy center with a teaspoon. Keep them in lemon water until use to avoid getting darken.

3. Transfer artichoke leaves to the pot with vegetable stock (or water) and other vegetables .Bring it to boil then simmer for 30-35 minutes.

4. Let it cool down for 20 minutes and strain through a fine strainer. Remove leaves.

6. Peel the skin of the broad beans one by one. (can be done overnight)

7. Add artichoke hearts and the artichoke stock in a stock pot bring it to boil and simmer until artichokes are tender.

8. Add broad beans to the pot and cook until very soft. Be careful not to overcook them. Otherwise, they lose the bright green color. We want them bright and vibrant.

9. Blend them until smooth, adjust seasoning. Add some lemon juice if desired. Cook for 2-3 minutes. Divide between bowls. Decorate with scarlet cress, basil flower, gangnam tops or whatever you prefer. Enjoy!

INGREDIENTS

350 gr. broad beans

1 large head artichoke

1 large red onion

2 large garlic cloves

1 large carrot

2 tbsp olive oil

750 ml. vegetable stock or water

Salt & Pepper to taste

A WONDERFULLY UNIQUE WAY TO USE IN-SEASON BROAD BEANS.

Bon Appetit

WITH CRACKERS & GARLIC CONFIT

CRACKERS

45 gr. flax seeds freshly grounded,

15 gr. white sesame seeds,

10 gr. poppy seeds,

15 gr. chia seeds,

15 gr. sunflower seeds,

Salt and pepper to taste

120 gr. warm water

DIRECTIONS

1. Mix all ingredients in a large bowl and add 125 ml. boiling water and mix well. Then let it rest for 15 minutes until absorbs all water.

2.Place the dough in between two baking paper and roll it evenly. It should be around 5-6 mm thick. Avoid making it too thin otherwise they crack during baking.

3. Remove the baking paper on top but keep the one underneath. Cut into long pieces.

4. Bake at 175 °C for about 8-10 minutes or until completely dry and crispy.

GARLIC CONFIT

70 gr. garlic

100 ml. olive oil

2 spring onion chives

1 spring thyme

DIRECTIONS

1.Place all ingredients in a sauce pot. Bring it to simmer but not boil.

2. Simmer at the lowest heat possible for about and hour. Garlic should be very soft but not caramelized.

3. Let it cool down. Strain the confit garlic but keep the oil. Mash garlic, transfer into a pipping bag. Decorate your crackers with little drops. *Garnish with scarlett cress & gangnam tops if desired.*

ALMOND CHEESE

Place soaked rinsed nuts into food processor, add probiotic powder and water. Mix on high speed until smooth. Transfer nut mixture into a nut milk bag. Gather up the ends to create a ball.

Wrap the ends and squeeze out any excess moisture. Place cheese in the dehydrator at 30 degrees for 24 hours to let it ferment. (House with an average temperature of 25-30°C for 24 hours.)

WITH PEPPERS, BEET AND LINGONBERRY

TIME
20 MINUTE

SERVING
6 PERSON

DIFFICULTY
10 / 7

Once the fermentation time is up, open the cheesecloth and observe your nut cheese very carefully. You will probably notice that a yellowish crust has formed on top. That is totally normal.

INGREDIENTS

Raw Almond Nuts	220 GR
Acidopholous Capsule	4 GR
Filtered Water	3 TBSP
Nutritional Yeast	1/2 TSP
Lemon Juice	75 ML
Sea Salt	1/2 TSP
Beetroot	1 SMALL
Dried Rosemary	4 TBSP
Pink Peppercorns	1/2 TSP
Lingonberry Powder	1 TBSP

TOPPINGS

A pinch of chili flakes, black and white sesame seeds.

DIRECTIONS

Cook beet until soften. Place into food processor, add a little warm water, blend until puree.

———

Place fermented almond into the food processor, add lemon juice, nutritional yeast, beet puree and salt. Mix on high speed until completely smooth. Form a log or ball on a piece of parchment paper and place in the fridge for 8-10 hours.

As you can consume the cheese next day, you can leave it to fermente for a week. The cheese will lost some water day by day, pat it dry with a paper towel if it is too wet and replace the parchment paper with new one. For the 2 next weeks, flip the cheese everyday and change the parchment paper regulary if it becomes wet.
At the end cover with beet, rosemary, pink peppercorns or lingonberry powder. Keep in the refrigerator.

PINK

ALMOND CHEESE

FRUITY

STUFFED CABBAGE

STUFFED CABBAGE

INGREDIENTS ———

Cabbage or Grape Leaves	500 GR
Olive Oil	1 CUP
Onion	1 MEDIUM
Rice	2 CUPS
Ground Cardamom	2 TSP
Sea Salt	1/2 TBSP
Lemon Juice	5 TBSP
Pine Nuts	50 GR
Lingonberries	1 CUP

METHOD	TIME	SERVING	DIFFICULTY
POT	85 MINUTE	6-8 PERSON	10/3

PREP

PLACE THE CABBAGE LEAVES IN BOILING WATER AND COOK FOR 10-12 MINUTES OR UNTIL SOFTEN. REMOVE FROM WATER, STRAIN AND SET ASIDE.

Heat olive oil, add onions and pine nuts in a large skillet, cook until fried. Add washed rice, salt and 1/2 cup hot water, stir for 3-4 minutes.

Add lemon juice and cardamom, stir and remove from the heat.

Fruity-tasting leaves that are perfect for anyone who loves the "alcoholic wine juice" called Arbor Mist.

DIRECTIONS

STEP I

Place a leaf with the stem toward on a flat surface. Cut out the stem of the leaf. Put a tablespoon filling and a pinch of lingonberries in the bottom center of the leaf. Roll the packet up toward the top point of the leaf. Place the rolls in layers in the cooking pot.

STEP II

Pour 1 cup hot water (cover them by about 1 inch), remaining lemon juice and olive oil over the rolls. Place an inverted heatproof plate on top of the rolls in order to keep them submerged in the water. Cook for 30 minutes on medium heat until rolls are tender. Drizzle olive oil, and serve with lemon if you prefer.

Bon Appetit

SPICY COCONUT BACON

OVEN   20 MINS   4 PERSON   10/4

It's easy-to-make, vegan, gluten free, and absolutely tasty!

INGREDIENTS

Fresh Coconut Meat	200 GR
Ground Coriander	1/2 TSP
Dried Tarragon	1/4 TSP
Nutritional Yeast	1 TBSP
Apple Cider Vinegar	1 TBSP
Tamari	1 TBSP
Smoked Paprika	1 TSP
Red Pepper	1/2 TBSP
Salt	1/2 TSP

STEP I Pre-heat oven to 175C. Place a parchment paper into the baking pan. Cut coconut meats into small pieces. Wash, strain and set aside. In a large bowl, mix all ingredients well. Add coconut meats into the bowl, toss together.

STEP II Place coconut meats onto the parchment paper, bake for 10 minutes or until flakes are golden brown. Then flip them and cook for about 10-12 minutes. If you need crispy, then cook for 15 minutes.

Let it cool and serve them with stir-fry veggies or salads.

You can keep them in the freezer up to 3 months.

HOW TO USE?

It's pretty amazing that you can replicate a baconish flavor and crispness with coconut flakes crunchy and savoury, these smokey "bacon" flavoured coconut strips will add an exciting twist to dishes!

JUST ADD

to your salads   to your sandwiches   over the soups

Bon Appetit

GREEN & AWAKE

RAW

HARISSA CARROT WRAPS

CARROT WRAPS

INGREDIENTS ————

50 gr. flaxseed meal

220 ml. filtered water

270 gr. carrot pulp

80 gr. red bell pepper
chopped

40 gr. cherry tomatoes
chopped

1 tbsp lemon juice

1/2 tsp harissa spice

1 tsp himalayan salt

METHOD	TIME	SERVING	DIFFICULTY
DEHYDRATOR	8-10 HOURS	4-5 PERSON	10/7

FOR THE VEGGIE FILLING:

THINLY SLICED PURPLE CABBAGE, GREEN COLLARDS, CUCUMBER, AVOCADO, PARSLEY, RED BELL PEPPER AND CULTURED CASHEW CREAM OR VEGAN TZATZIKI SAUCE.

DIRECTIONS

1. Blend all the ingredients in a blender or food processor until very smooth. The consistency should be fluid.

2. Spread mixture onto the parchment sheets approximately 4 mm (3/16 inch) thick using a angled spatula.

3. Dehydrate at 41°C (106°F) for 7-8 hours, or until the exposed side has set and is firm enough for you to peel away from the sheets. Flip the wrap onto a mesh tray and peel back the sheets. If you need, dehydrate for a further 1-2 hours or until completely dry but still pliable. (You should be careful and do not to over-dry the wraps. If the wraps become too dry and start cracking around the edges)

4. Once ready, cut each sheet into 2-4 pieces using a sharp knife, depending on how large you like your wrap. Store them in single layers in an air-tight container with parchment paper between each layer to prevent sticking in the refrigerator up to 2-3 weeks.

5. To roll them, place 4-5 green collard leaves onto the carrot wraps.

6. Slice veggies very thinly according to your preference, place onto the collard leaves, spread cashew cream, sesame seeds and roll it carefully. Enjoy!

Bon Appetit

PHYLLO PASTRY

Phyllo (also spelled filo), which means "leaf" in Greek, is tissue-thin sheets of dough that have very little fat. Many popular Turkish and Greek dishes, such as baklava and spanakopita, are made with phyllo dough. The sheets are usually brushed with oil and then layered together. When it bakes up, the layers get airy, crisp, and flaky.

HOW TO ENJOY IT

The main thing to know about working with phyllo dough is to keep it from drying out.

Keep the sheets covered with a towel while you're working!

STEP 1

Lightly fry onions and garlic cloves in a little walnut oil. Fry on medium heat for 4-5 minutes and add chopped chili, salt, tomato and spinach. Cook until excess water has evaporated. Set aside.

In a medium bowl, stir together almond milk and 1 tbsp walnut oil.

Ingredient	Amount
Spinach	400 GR
Onion	1 MEDIUM
Carrot	1 SMALL
Red Pepper	2 MEDIUM
Phyllo Dough	8 THIN SHEETS
Almond Milk	1 CUP
Soy Sauce	2 TBSP
Olive Oil	4 TBSP

STEP 2

Place a sheet dough on the bottom of the baking pan. Spread soy milk sauce until completely wet. Lightly brush sheet with the spinach mixture using a small pastry brush. Lay another sheet of phyllo dough on top, brush with almond milk mixture.

STEP 3

Add one more layer and repeat process for the remaining 5 sheets too.
Brush soy milk oil mixture on top floor until full wet. Spread black and white sesame seeds.

Bake in pre-heat oven to 250 degrees for 30 minutes or till golden brown. Cut in triangles and serve warm!

To freeze: prepare, fill the pastry. Do not coat with liquid wash or bake. Place the unbaked pastries in a pyrex separating each layer of pastry with a piece of parchment paper to keep them from freezing together. Freeze. When ready to bake, take the pastry out of the freezer and arrange them on a baking sheet sprayed with nonstick oil. Coat with thin layer of plant based milk wash and sesame or poppy seeds, if desired. Bake at 250 degrees for 20-30 minutes till golden brown.

Bon Appetit

SPINACH
TRIANGLES

METHOD
OVEN

TIME
50 MINUTE

SERVING
4 PERSON

DIFFUCULTY
10 / 5

GREEN & AWAKE

ARTICHOKE

WITH PINEAPPLE

ARTICHOKE WITH PINEAPPLE

INGREDIENTS

Artichoke Hearts	4 PIECES
Carrot	1 MEDIUM
Fresh Peas	1 CUP
Pineapple	2 SLICES
Pineapple Juice	1/2 CUP
Sea Salt	A PINCH
Lemon Juice	1 TBSP
Coconut Sugar	1 TBSP
Warm Water	4 TBSP

METHOD POT

TIME 30 MINUTE

SERVING 4 PERSON

DIFFICULTY 10/3

BE THE CHANGE USE JUICY PINEAPPLE INSTEAD OF POTATOES

It is a spring-summer dish that is very popular in Aegean region of Turkey and in Greece.

DIRECTIONS

STEP I

Cut carrots and pineapples into small pieces. Add peas, transfer them in a pan and cook for 6-7 minutes on medium heat.
Mix coconut sugar, pineapple juice and lemon juice and split in half. Sauce is ready!

STEP II

Cut carrots and pineapples into small pieces. Add peas, transfer all of them in a pan and cook for 6-7 minutes on medium heat
Put carrot, pineapple and peas mixture on the artichoke. Cook for 5 minutes. Pour over remaining sauce and serve warm or cold.

Bon Appetit

CELERY ROOT HASHBROWNS

METHOD
PAN

TIME
30 MINS

SERVING
3-4 PERSON

DIFFICULTY
10/4

INGREDIENTS

Celery Root	1 LARGE
Potato	1 LARGE
Chili Pepper	1/2 TSP
Fresh Basil Leaves	5-6 LEAVES
Baking Soda	A PINCH
Whole Wheat Flour	4 TBSP
Lupin Powder (or flax seeds)	2 TSP
Water	6 TSP
Olive Oil	TO FRY

PREP Wash the celery roots and potato. Grate them over a large bowl. Wash, drain and cut basil leaves into small pieces. n a small bowl, mix lupin powder with water well.

STEP I Add chili pepper, cutted basil leaves, baking soda, whole wheat flour, lupin mixture and salt into the bowl. Mix with grated celery potato mixture. Knead with your hands well.

STEP II Pour the olive oil into the frying pan until the bottom of the pan is just coated in oil. Heat the pan over medium-high heat and add 1 tablespoon of the hashbrown mixture, flattening it and evenly spreading it out over the surface of the pan with a spatula. Fry for 5-6 minutes on each side, until golden brown. When they are fried, remove the hashbrown patties from the pan and place it on a plate lined with paper towels.

SERVE WARM OR COLD WITH CHILI SAUCE

W I T H   C H I L I

EASY CHILI SAUCE

Whisk tomato sauce, brown sugar, vinegar, chili powder, garlic powder, and onion powder together in a bowl.

INGREDIENTS

1 cup tomato sauce

1 tablespoon coconut sugar

1/4 teaspoon garlic powder

2 tablespoons distilled white vinegar

1/2 teaspoon chili powder

1/4 teaspoon onion powder

—————— ADD EXTRA RED CHILI POWDER IF DESIRED ——————

MOONG DAL CHILLA

WITH GREEN CHUTNEY & AVOCADO

MUNG BEAN CREPES

Just like Dosa in South India, Chilla is an absolute favourite Breakfast recipe in North India. Almost every North Indian household makes Chilla for breakfast with a hot cup of tea or coffee or sometimes even for lunch during weekdays, as it is extremely easy to make and nutritious too.

AN INDIAN PANCAKE WITH A CREATIVE TWIST

TIME
45 MINUTE

SERVING
5 PERSON

DIFFICULTY
10 / 4

GREEN CHUTNEY

1 cup chopped coriander leaves,

1 green chili,

1/ 2 tsp ginger puree,

1/2 lemon juice,

1/4 teaspoon salt

It is not only high in protein, but Moong Dal also has many health benefits, such as it has a low glycemic index, rich in fibre and these properties help to regulate blood sugar for diabetics.

INGREDIENTS

1 cup mung lentils soaked overnight,

1 small onion,

4-5 cherry tomatoes,

1 tsp garlic puree,

1 medium red bell pepper,

1 tsp ginger puree,

1/4 tsp turmeric,

1/2 tsp salt,

2 tbsp olive oil

1/2 avocado ,

Sesame and coriander leaves to decorate

DIRECTIONS

1. Place mung beans into the water overnight and soak at least 6 hours. Then rinse and drain them.
2. Place mung beans into the food processor, add all remaining ingredients (expect from avocado) and blend on high speed until you get smooth mixture.
3. Once the mixture is smooth, heat and spread some olive oil on the pan.
4. Pour it on the pan evenly.
5. Cook on slow to medium heat for about a minute. Then flip the side and cook for another minute until crispy.
6. Repeat the process for to make more chillas.
7. Place all chutney ingredients into the food processor mix on high speed until puree. Then pour mixture over the crepes.
8. Peel a lightly ripe avocado (shouldn't be soft) using a standart peeler. Roll them with your hands and give a rose shape. Top on the chutney.
9. Sprinkle some sesame and coriander leaves , serve!

GREEN & AWAKE

WILD PURSLANE

ENDIVE SALAD

This is a very good salad combination that makes even the simplest plate of greens memorable.

Purslane has been said to be one of the most nutrient rich greens on earth! According to researchers , it actually has the highest amount of heart-healthy omega-3 fats of any edible plant. They also reported that this herb has 10 to 20 times more melatonin — a hormone naturally released in our body that helps regulate sleep and natural body rhythms — than any other fruit or vegetable tested and amazingly enough, it is also getting the spotlight for its cancer prevention properties and ability to inhibit the growth of cancer cells.

Some herbalists believe that these delicious wild greens naturally grow at this time of year so that we can gather them and use them to cleanse the body. If you are lucky and see them at farmer market. They are also perfect for starting a spring cleanse!

ENDIVE WILD PURSLANE SALAD

INGREDIENTS ———

METHOD
RAW

TIME
15 MIN

SERVING
2-3 PERSON

DIFFICULTY
10/2

Salad Ingredients:

2 heads endive chopped

4 cups purslane

1 cup radish microgreens

1/2 cup scralet cress

4-5 fresh physalis halved

Hemp hearts for topping (optional)

1/2 cup gangnam tops (optional)

White violet flower (optional)

For the vinaigrette:

1 tbsp extra virgin olive oil

1 tsp dijon mustard

1 tbsp red wine vinegar

A pinch of salt and pepper

DIRECTIONS

1. To prepare endive for salads, first remove the dense, crunchy core: Using a paring knife, halve the endive lengthwise and make two angled cuts along the outside of the core. Pull out and discard the core, and then slice. Place in a large bowl.

2. Wash your purslane, gangam tops and microgreens. Transfer to the bowl.

3. Add vinaigrette ingredients into a small bowl. Whisk well until well combined.

4. Toss with greens and top with hemp hearts and halved physalis.

Bon Appetit

POT

25 MINS

4 PERSON

10/3

a comforting winter dish

GREEN & AWAKE

INGREDIENTS

1 medium head cauliflower (approx. 550 gr),

2 leeks,

5-6 garlic cloves,

4 tbsp olive oil,

3-4 fresh sage leaves,

1/4 tsp white pepper,

600 ml water

Crumble Topping:

4 tbsp pine nuts,

2 tbsp walnuts,

1 tbsp nutritional yeast

6-7 sage leaves,

2 tbsp olive oil,

A pinch of salt and black pepper

DIRECTIONS

STEP I

Cut leeks into small pieces, add in a large pan. Add some olive oil and fry until golden. Add garlic and sauté for 3 more minutes. Then add fresh sage, salt and pepper. In a large pot, cover cauliflower with water and bring to boil until soften.

STEP II

Transfer mixture from pan to blender. Add some water depending on your blender and how liquid you like. I added 600 ml water.
Blend mixture until silky smooth. Then transfer to a deep pot. Taste it, if it is too thick, then add more water and salt. Then cook for 3-4 minutes on medium heat.

STEP III

To make the Pine Nut crumble, place all ingredients expect olive oil into a small food processor. Pulse several times until it is roughly chopped. Heat olive oil in a skillet over medium heat and gently toast the crumble, stirring constantly for about 5 minutes until golden and fragrant. Season with salt and pepper.

CAULIFLOWER SOUP

SAGE & PINE NUTS

ROASTED ZUCCIHINI FLOWERS WITH CASHEW CHEESE

METHOD
OVEN

TIME
40 MINS

SERVING
4-5

ZUCCHINI FLOWERS ARE A DELICIOUS AND VIBRANT DELICACY USED IN TRADITIONAL ITALIAN COOKING

INGREDIENTS

Zucchini Flowers	10-12
Raw Cashews	1 CUP
Olive Oil	1 TBSP
Basil Leaves	5-6
Nutritional Yeast	1/2 TBSP
Almond Milk	2 TBSP
Lemon Juice	1/2
Salt	1/2 TSP
Thyme	A PINCH
Pepper	A PINCH

DIRECTIONS

Wash and remove the stamens of zucchini flowers. Drain and set aside. To make filling, place cashews into the food processor, mix on high speed until get flour. Then add, almond milk, lemon juice, salt, basil leaves and mix until smooth. Carefully fill zucchini flowers with pesto cheese. Place a parchment paper on to the baking tray. Place stuffed zucchini flowers. Drizzle with olive oil, sprinkle thyme and peppers. Bake at 200 degrees for 15 minutes or until golden browned. Serve with ketchup or your favorite sauce.

Bon Appetit

The edible flower of the courgette, or zucchini bush. There are two sorts of flower: the flower with the immature vegetable attached is the female and the more eyecatching flower on the long stalk is the male. It is the male flower that is sold in bunches and used in Italian cooking.

If you see courgette flowers, snap them up - some supermarkets and most greengrocers stock them over the summer.

SALADS

FROM SIDE DISH TO STAR ATTRACTION, NO MENU IS COMPLETE WITHOUT A SALAD

Whether you're looking for hearty main dish salad recipes or light, nutritious fare, these salads are far from ordinary.

GREEN & AWAKE

SALAD

WITH LEMONY WALNUT DRESSING

BEET BUCKWHEAT KALE

INGREDIENTS ———

Beet Chopped Thinly	1 MEDIUM
Buckwheat cooked	1/2 CUP
Kale Finely Chopped	100 GR
Fresh Mint	A HANDFUL
Walnut Chopped	1/2 CUP
Dried Figs (Optional)	A HANDFUL

TIME
15 MINUTE

SERVING
2 PERSON

DIFFICULTY
10/3

DRESSING ———

Lemon Juice	1 MEDIUM
Walnuts	A HANDFUL
Hemp or Avocado Oil	1 TBSP
Sea Salt	1/2 TSP
Water	TO THIN

DIRECTIONS

STEP I

Place chopped kale leaves to a bowl, add cooked buckwheast. (You can also add activated & dehydrated buckwheats if you would like to make this recipe raw.)
Add thinly chopped beets.

STEP II

Spread fresh mint leaves, chopped walnut and dried figs to the bowl. Mix with veggies.

STEP III

Place all dressing ingredients into the food processor, mix on high speed until smooth.
Pour mixture over the salad. Massage with your hands or give it a good toss. Serve!

Bon Appetit

BELUGA LENTIL

PREPARATION

First slice your potato and carrot into cubes. Then bring to boil in warm water until soften. Set aside. Place 1 cup water and beluga lentil into the deep pot, bring to boil for 20 minutes. Strain and set aside.

FULL OF NUTRITIOUS SALAD WITH NUTS AND FRUITS

TIME	SERVING	DIFFICULTY
20 MINUTE	4 PERSON	10 / 4

INGREDIENTS

Leek sliced thinly	1 LARGE
Provence Herbs	2 TSP
Beluga Lentil	1 CUP
Pomegranate Syrup	2 TBSP
Pumpkin Seeds	2 TBSP
Salt and Pepper	TO TASTE
Lemon Juice	4 TBSP
Ginger Powder	1 TSP
Maple Syrup	2 TBSP
Olive Oil	3 TBSP
Brussels Sprouts	300 GR
Walnuts	A HANDFUL
Incaberries	1/2 CUP
Fresh Rosemary	A HANDFUL
Baby Spinach Leaves	A HANDFUL

DIRECTIONS

1. Finely chop leeks and brussel sprouts, add to a pan. On low-medium heat cook until soften stirring occasionaly. Add some water in order to prevent sticking to the pan. You can also add olive oil if desired. But scientists found that heating up vegetable oils led to the release of high concentrations of chemicals called aldehydes, which have been linked to illnesses including cancer, heart disease and dementia. So It is best to cook with water as much as we can do.

2. To make dressing, in a bowl mix pomegranate syrup, lemon juice, salt, pepper, ginger powder, maple syrup, olive oil together. Set aside.

3. In a large bowl, add washed and drained baby spinach leaves, add cooked beluga lentil on top, add cooked brussel sprouts and leeks. Then add walnuts, fresh rosemary and halved incaberries.

4. Pour dressing over the salad. Toss well with all ingredients. Spread pumkin seeds. Divide between bowls. Taste it, adjust seasonsing if desired. Enjoy!

Bon Appetit

BELUGA LENTIL

BRUSSELS SPROUTS

KALE & SPICY CHICKPEAS

OVEN   50 MINS   2-3 PERSON   10/4

SALAD INGREDIENTS

Kale Leaves	1 LARGE BUNDLE
Grapeseed Oil	1 TBSP
Lemon Juice	2 TBSP
Salt	1/2 TSP
Beet	1 SMALL
Crispy Fried Onions	3-4 TBSP

SPICY CHICKPEA SAUCE

Chickpeas	1 CUP
Grapeseed Oil	3 TBSP
Paprika	1 TSP
Dried Thyme	1 TSP
Ground Turmeric	1/2 TSP
Coriander	1/4 TSP
Red Pepper Flakes	1/2 TSP
Cardamom, Cinnamon	1/4 TSP

STEP I

Pre-heat oven to 200C. n a large bowl, mix all chickpea sauce ingredients well. Add chickpeas into the bowl, stir to combine well. Place a parchment paper in the baking tray. Transfer chickpeas here. Bake for 25 minutes or until crispy enough.

STEP II

Wash and rinse kale leaves, cut into 2-3 small pieces. Place in a large bowl. Pour almond caesar sauce (see on right page) and massage with your hands to soften and coat the kale for about 1-2 minutes.

When chickpeas are fried, spread them onto the salad. Add grated beets. Spread some crispy fried onion. Add salt, lemon and juice if you need. Enjoy!

WITH ALMOND CAESAR SAUCE

HOW TO MAKE ALMOND CAESAR?

Place all ingrediengts into the food processor, mix on high speed until silky. Add some water as you need to thin the mixture.

INGREDIENTS

2 cloves of garlic,
3-4 tablespoons lemon juice,
A pinch of blackpepper

1 teaspoon dried mint,
1/ tablespoon maple syrup,
A pinch of sea salt

1/4 cup water to thin,
80 gr. raw almonds pre-soaked

MASSAGE WELL WITH KALE LEAVES

GREEN & AWAKE

CHILI CARROT

WITH QUINOA

CHILI CARROT

INGREDIENTS ———

Quinoa cooked	1/2 CUP
Beluga Lentil	1/4 CUP
Colorful Carrots	2 LARGE
Red Onion Thinly Sliced	1 LARGE
Garlic Powder	1 TSP
Turmeric Powder	1 TSP
Paprika	1 TSP
Chopped Walnuts	1/2 CUP
Salt and Pepper	1/4 TSP
Olive Oil	1/4 CUP
Microgreens	TO DECORATE
Chili Sauce	1 TSP

METHOD
OVEN

TIME
15 MINS

SERVING
2-3

DIFFICULTY
10/3

THESE SHAVED CARROTS WITH CHILI PEPPER AND WALNUTS ARE A CRUNCHY SALAD WITH A BIT OF SPICE.

Be aware: White or golden carrots are typically a yellow or cream color. These vegetables have a mild flavor with hardly any of the earthiness that the other colors of carrots typically contain. These types of carrots are also notably sweeter than orange, red, and purple carrots.

DIRECTIONS

STEP I

Pre-heat oven to 200 degrees, line tray with parchment paper. Set aside cooked quinoa and beluga lentil. Cut carrots and onions thinly. Mix rest of the ingredients expect walnuts, microgreens and rosemary together. Then coat carrots with the sauce well.

STEP II

Spread veggies onto baking tray evenly and roast for about 25 minutes. Place cooked quinoa and beluga lentil in a bowl, add walnuts, rosemary, salt and pepper. Toss together.

STEP III

When carrots are fried, then add into the bowl, mix with quinoa mixture. Drizzle some olive oil if you need. Give it a good toss and serve with micro greens.

Bon Appetit

EVERYDAY SALAD

TIME	**SERVING**	**DIFFICULTY**
45 MINUTE	2-3	10 / 2

easy to make

A PERFECT WAY OF ENJOYING SALAD EVERYDAY

This Salad is one of my favorite go-to recipes when I am looking to whip up a big batch of healthy. The salad is comprised entirely of fresh produce, without being drenched in any fatty dressings. The dressing consists simply of lime juice,vinegar, salt, and pepper. Simple, but yet incredibly flavorful.

INGREDIENTS

Purslane	200 GR
Avocado	1 RIPE
Black Beans	1/2 CUP
Pumpkin Seeds	4 TBSP
Lemon Juice	2 TBSP
Tamari	3 TBSP
Sea Salt	1 TSP
Chopped Onion	1 SMALL
Green & Red Peppers	2-3
Ground Mustard	1 TSP
Olive Oil	1 TBSP
Garlic Powder	1 TSP
Balsamic Vinegar	1 TSP

DIRECTIONS

Wash, strain and drain purslane florets, set aside.

———————————

Peel, remove the seed of avocado and slice into cubes. Add lemon juice and sprinkle salt. Set aside.

Wash and strain your beans. Cover with filtered water, bring to boil for 30 minutes or until soften. In a large skillet pan, heat olive oil, add chopped onions, peppers and cook until soften, then add ground mustard, garlic powder and soy sauce. Transfer beans into the skillet. Cook on medium heat for 4-5 minutes.

Place purslane florets into the plate, add beans and spread avocado cubes. Drizzle with balsamic vinegar. Serve warm or cold.

Bon Appetit

EVERYDAY SALAD

WITH PURSLANE, AVOCADO AND BEANS

KALE & POTATO WITH

If you're looking to sneak a healthy meal in between all the indulgence but not willing to sacrifice big taste, this warm salad is exactly what you need! With hearty roasted potatoes, cashews and dinosaur kale the salad is so delicious and satisfying that you'll forget that things like Christmas cookies even exist. At least for a quick minute.

INGREDIENTS

Potato	2 MEDIUM
Zucchini	1 LARGE
Kale de-stalked	100 GR
Macadamia Oil	3 TBSP
Colorful Peppers	2-3
Onion Chopped	1 MEDIUM
Ginger Powder	1 TSP
Coriander	1 TSP
Tangerine Juice	1/4 CUP
Curry Powder	2 TSP
Cherry Tomatoes	1 CUP
Broccoli	1 MEDIUM HEAD
Cashews	70 GR

STEP 1

Pre-heat oven to 200 degrees. Peel and cut potatoes and zucchini into chunks. Place onto the baking tray with oily sheet. Spread 1 tbsp macadamia oil over them. Roast them for 30-40 minutes until golden browned.

STEP 2

To make vegetable mix, chop broccoli, onions and yellow, red, green capsicums and add them into a pan, caramelize with 2 tbsp macadamia oil for 5-6 minutes. To make curry sauce, in a small bowl mix coriander, curry, salt, tangerine juice and ginger.

STEP 3

Place kale pieces in a large pan, drizzle 1 tbsp macadamia oil, and pour 1 tbsp curry mix sauce over them. Toss on high heat for 3-4 minutes. Set aside. Pour remaining curry sauce over the vegetable mix, stir and mix well. In a small pot, mix cashews with 1 tsp chili pepper and 1 tbsp water until fried. Remove baking tray from the oven, let cool for 10-15 minutes.

Place roasted zucchini and potatoes in a plate. Add vegetable mix and kale leaves.
Top with cashews. Serve with cooked quinoa or black wild rice if desired.

Bon Appetit

CURRY
S A U C E

METHOD	**TIME**	**SERVING**	**DIFFICULTY**
OVEN	55 MINUTE	3-4	10 / 5

BLUEBERRY MUNG BEAN

This dish can be served both cold and hot and preserves flavor in both ways. So it is very easy to carry it in a bowl during your trips.

INGREDIENTS

Ingredient	Amount
Mung Beans	1 CUP
Onion Chopped	1 MEDIUM
Sea Salt	1 TSP
Olive Oil	2 TBSP
Cashews	A HANDFUL
Parsley	1/2 BUNCH
Colorful Peppers	3-4
Tamari	2 TBSP
Maple Syrup	1 TBSP
Tangerine Juice	1 CUP
Blueberry	50 GR

STEP 1

Wash mung beans and strain. Place into a large port, cover with water. Bring to boil on medium heat for 20 minutes or until lightly soften.

STEP 2

Saute sliced onions in the olive oil or water (if you are avoiding to heat oil). Cut peppers into very small pieces, add to pan. Add maple syrup, tangerine juice, cashews, blueberries, tamari, and salt. Cook on medium heat until caramelized well.

STEP 3

When mung beans are soften, add them into the pan.

Occasionally stirring, cook it on medium heat for around 3-4 minutes.

Sprinkle fresh mint leaves or parsley on top. Serve cold or warm!

Bon Appetit

MUNG
B E A N

METHOD
POT

TIME
50 MINUTE

SERVING
4 PERSON

DIFFICULTY
10 / 3

RAINBOW SALAD

ROASTED VEGGIES & QUINOA

ROASTED VEGGIES & QUINOA

INGREDIENTS ———

METHOD	**TIME**	**SERVING**	**DIFFICULTY**
OVEN	50 MINUTE	2-3	10/3

Butternut Squash	100 GR
Broccoli Head	1 LARGE
Turmeric	1 TSP
Sea Salt	1/8 TSP
Beluga Lentil Cooked	50 GR
Kale Leaves Chopped	100 GR
Swiss Chard Leaves	2 LARGE
Sesame Seeds	1 TBSP

AVOCADO DRESSING

1 Large Avocado

1/2 Lemon Juice

1/8 Teaspoon Salt

3-4 Cherry Tomatoes

1 Small Garlic Minced

1/3 Teaspoon Ground Mustard

1 Small Jalapeno

DIRECTIONS

STEP I

Pre-heat the oven to 200 degrees and place a parchment paper to a large roasting tray and add the olive oil. Add the butternut squash and toss in the oil. Roast for 10 minutes. Cut broccoli heads into small florets. Then add the broccoli with the spices, salt and pepper. Roast for a further 20 minutes.

STEP II

Meanwhile, add the cooked quinoa and lentils to a large bowl and mix in the kale and swiss chard leaves. Once the veggies are cooked and cooled slightly, mix into the salad with the leaves, quinoa and lentils.

STEP III

Place all sauce ingredients into the food processor, mix on high speed. Pour over the salad. Sprinkle sesame seeds.

Bon Appetit

SHIITAKE QUINOA LENTIL

GREAT SOURCE OF B12

Obtaining sufficient amounts of vitamin B12 is essential for every cell in the body as it plays a key role in DNA replication. The recommended daily intake of vitamin B12 is 2.4mg per day to ensure a wide range of health benefits including energy production, regulation of the nervous the system, reduction of cardiovascular disease, encouraging optimal digestion and essential for hair, skin and nails. Shitake mushrooms may prove to be the most beneficial in vegan diets as dried shiitake mushrooms are around 5.6mg per 100 gm dried weight. This means that the daily intake of approximately 50gm of dried shiitake mushroom will meet the 2.4mg/day for the average adult.

TIME
40 MINUTE

SERVING
3 PERSON

DIFFICULTY
10 / 3

b12 Source

The quinoa adds protein as well as a chewy texture to this hearty dish.

INGREDIENTS

Shiitake Mushrooms	100	GR
Strawberries	1/2	CUP
Chili Pepper	2-3	
Asparagus	5	BRANCH
Leek	1/2	LONG
Fresh Dill	1/2	BUNCH
Quinoa	1/2	CUP
Green Lentil	1/4	CUP
Soy Sauce	2	TBSP
Olive Oil	1	TBSP
Mustard Powder	1/2	TSP
Lime	3-4	TBSP

DIRECTIONS

Place quinoa and green lentils in a pot, cover with water. Bring to boil on medium heat for 20 minutes.

In a large pan, add olive oil and soy sauce. Sauté sliced shiitakes, asparagus, leek and chili peppers on high heat stirring constantly.
When veggies are sautéed then add garlic powder, thyme, mustard powder, mix well.
When quinoa lentil mixture are cooked, strain, drain and add to the pan. Mix with veggies and cook for 2- 4 minutes.

Add strawberry slices and chopped fresh dill onto the pilaf. Give it a good toss. Serve warm with lime slices if desired.

Bon Appetit

WARM SALAD

S H I I T A K E   Q U I N O A   L E N T I L

GREEN & AWAKE

TABOULI

S W E E T   T E M P E S T   B O W L

T A B O U L I

I N G R E D I E N T S ———

Fine Bulgur Wheat	200 GR
Cherry Tomatoes	7 LARGE
Colorful Peppers	2 TBSP
Parsley, Dill, Mint	1 MEDIUM
Lemon Juice	2 TBSP
Green Onion	60 GR
Walnuts	2 MEDIUM
Strawberry	2 TBSP
Pomegranate Syrup	1 TSP

METHOD	TIME	SERVING	DIFFICULTY
OVEN	15 MINS	3 PERSON	10/1

P R E P

THIS IS THE PERFECT EASY SIDE DISH FOR YOUR FAVORITE MIDDLE EASTERN COOKING.

Aside from the olive oil in the dressing the dish is full of vitamins from the fresh ingredients.

Fine bulgur is a great that doesn't require cooking. It soaks in water until softened before being eaten.

D I R E C T I O N S

STEP I

Wash your bulgur well, strain and set aside. Chop peppers, dill, onion and parsley very finely. Place in a bowl.

STEP II

Transfer bulgur in to the greens, mix together.

STEP III

Add cherry tomatoes, lime juice, salt, walnuts, strawberries and pomegranate syrup. Give it a good toss.
Serve cold for the best result.

Bon Appetit

SWEET PEA & QUINOA

The cool thing about stir fry is that it's one of the most flexible meals you can make. You can pretty much toss in whatever combination of veggies.

INGREDIENTS

Quinoa	1 CUP	
Asparagus	6-7 HALVED	
Sweet Peas	1/2 CUP	
Radish	1 SMALL	
Broccoli Head	1 SMALL	
Mint & Dill	1/3 BUNCH	
Tamari	2 TBSP	
Olive Oil	2 TBSP	
Sea Salt	1/2 TSP	
Maple Syrup	1 TBSP	
Onion & Garlic	1/2 TSP	
Green Pepper	3-4 MEDIUM	

STEP 1

Heat olive oil & soy sauce in a large skillet pan. add asparagus, broccoli, and peppers, fry on high heat stirring occasionally until crispy. Add sweet peas and sprinkle salt, onion and garlic powder. Cook for about 3-4 minutes. If you need add 1 tablespoon water.

Then they are tender, add maple syrup, stir well.

STEP 2

Wash and strain quinoa, cover with water and cook until soften for about 20 minutes.
Transfer cooked quinoa into the pan, combine with veggies well.

STEP 3

Serve with cherry tomatoes and sliced radish.
Spread sesame seeds, fresh dill and mint leaves.

Serve cold or warm!

Bon Appetit

STIR-FRY

ASPARAGUS & PEPPERS

TIME
40 MINS

SERVING
2-3

DIFFICULTY
10 / 3

AVOCADO PITAYA CAPRESE

WHAT IS CAPRESE?

This traditional Italian summer salad originates from the Isle of Capri in the Gulf of Naples, Italy. Caprese literally means from Capri.

THIS SIMPLE SALAD RECIPE IS FAST AND FRESH

TIME
20 MINUTE

SERVING
6 PERSON

DIFFICULTY
10 / 2

refreshing

It is is so easy to make and uses fresh ingredients but you can also grill tomatoes, pitaya, avocado and walnuts if you like.

INGREDIENTS

Pitaya	100 GR
Pomegranate Syrup	50 ML
Cherry Tomato	130 GR
Avocado	1 RIPE
Fresh Basil chiffonade cut	5-6 LEAVES
Olive Oil	1 TBSP
Lemon Juice	1 TSP
Walnut chopped	A HANDFUL
Sesame Seeds	1 TSP
Salt	1/4 TSP

DIRECTIONS

Peel pitaya and cut into cubes. Cut tomatoes half. Add pitaya cubes, tomatoes, avocado, fresh basil into a large bowl.

Drizzle on the oil and lemon juice. Then gently toss the veggies are coated. Season generously with salt and pepper and toss just briefly. Scatter on desired amount seeds and walnuts, drizzle on all of the pomegranate syrup.

Bon Appetit

CAPRESE

AVOCADO & PITAYA

GRAPEFRUIT FENNEL SALAD

WITH AVOCADO

GRAPEFRUIT FENNEL SALAD

INGREDIENTS ———

2 pink grapefruit peeled, cut into chunks,

2 avocados peeled, cut into chunks,

1 fennel bulb thinly sliced,

Raw vegan parmesan to sprinkle (optional but recommended)

Sprouted amaranth, peas, broccoli & violet (optional to decorate)

METHOD	TIME	SERVING	DIFFICULTY
RAW	15 MINS	2- 3	10/1

DRESSING ———

2 tbsp lemon juice

1 tbsp extra virgin olive oil,

2 tbsp minced shallot,

1 tbsp balsamic vinegar,

1 tsp mustard (optional),

1/4 tsp salt

1/4 tsp ground black pepper

DIRECTIONS

STEP I

Combine the fennel, avocado, grapefruits and greens in a large bowl or plate.

STEP II

Add all of the dressing ingredients into a bowl, whisk well until smooth.

STEP III

Drizzle with 3-4 tablespoons of the citrus dressing and season with the salt and pepper, top with vegan parmesan. Enjoy!

Bon Appetit

CREAMY CUCUMBER SALAD

SOUR CASHEW YOGURT

Raw Cashews	200	GR
Probiotic	2	CAPSULES
Filtered Water	130	ML
Sea Salt	1/4	TSP
Lemon Juice	3	TBSP
Dried Peppermint	1/4	TSP

SALAD INGREDIENTS

English Cucumber	2	LARGE
Sour Cashew Yogurt	1/2	CUP
Fresh Dill	1/2	BUNCH
Sea Salt	A PINCH	
Lemon Juice	1/2	
Black Sesame	2	TBSP
Minced Garlic Clove	1/2	

STEP I Soak cashews overnight. Strain and place in a high speed blender. Add water and probiotic capsules. Mix on high speed until you get silky smooth mixture.

STEP II Transfer mixture in a bowl, cover with a kitchen towel. Dehydrate for 8-10 hours at 30 ° C

After fermentation process , add salt, mint and lemon juice. If the mixture is too thick, add 2-3 tbsp water to thin and stir welll. Transfer in a mason jar.

Store in the refrigerator for up to 2-3 days.

STEP I Peel the cucumber and slice in half length-ways or using a spiral cutter make cucumber noodles.

STEP II Place cucumber to a large bowl.

Chop the dill finely , stir the lemon juice, yoghurt and minced garlic.

Pour mixture over the cucumber. Toss together. Sprinkle black sesame seeds. Serve cold with raw crackers if you prefer.

WITH YOGURT

TIME
40 MINS

SERVING
2-3

DIFFICULTY
10 / 3

PROVENCAL

WITH COWPEA AND KIWI

PROVENCAL SALAD

INGREDIENTS ———

Cowpea	100 GR
Provence Greens	200 GR
Olive Oil	4 TBSP
Onion Chopped	1 MEDIUM
Tamari	2 TBSP
Rosemary, Thyme, Mint	A PINCH
Jalapeno	3 MEDIUM
Kiwi	6-7 SLICES
Tomatoes	1/2 CUP
Pomegranate Syrup	2 TBSP

METHOD	TIME	SERVING	DIFFICULTY
POT	20 MINS	3 PERSON	10/2

PREP

PLACE PEAS IN A POT, COVER WITH WATER BY 2-3 INCHES. BRING TO BOIL ON LOW HEAT UNTIL PEAS ARE TENDERED, BUT NOT MUSHY. AFTER 20-30 MINUTES, STRAIN THE PEAS AND SET ASIDE.

Chop your greens, thinly slice onion and peppers, cut kiwi slices into small chunks, divide tomatoes half.

Provencal salad that traditionally mix includes chervil, arugula, leafy lettuces and endive in equal proportions.

DIRECTIONS

STEP I

Add olive oil, garlic, chopped jalapeño, onion and tamari in a pan on medium heat. Mix them for 4-5 minutes until they are soften.

STEP II

Add parsley, rosemary, thyme, mint, dill, lime juice and salt, stir on high heat for 1-2 minutes. Pour the beans into the pan and mix with caramelized vegetables.

STEP III

Cut the Provence greens by bamboo knife and place in a large bowl. Add beans mixture on top of the greens.
Place pickles and tomatoes. Dress with lime juice, pomegranate syrup and olive oil. Add sliced kiwi.

Bon Appetit

BRUSSELS SPROUTS

Brussels sprouts are named after Brussels, Belgium, where it is believed they were first widely cultivated in the 16th century. Sometimes called mini cabbages, they have appeared on "most hated vegetable" lists due to their potentially bitter flavors caused by sulfur-containing compounds. Overcooking the vegetable, particularly by boiling, will intensify any bitter flavors and unpleasant odors. However, when properly cooked and seasoned, Brussels sprouts offer a natural, nutty sweetness.

TIME	SERVING	DIFFUCULTY
20 MINUTE	3 PERSON	10 / 3

Holiday Dish

Brussels sprouts roasted to perfection in pure maple are the perfect addition to your holiday table.

INGREDIENTS

Brussels Sprouts	150 GR
Pomegranate Syrup	2 TBSP
Olive Oil	2 TBSP
Maple Syrup	1 TBSP
Balsamic Vinegar	1 TBSP
Mustard Powder	1 TSP
Garlic Powder	1 TSP
Pomegranate Seeds	1/2 CUP
Pecan Nut	1/2 CUP
Fresh Mint	6-7 LEAVES

DIRECTIONS

In a large wok pan, heat oil, add halved brussel sprouts, pecan nuts and a little bit water, cook on medium heat until lightly fried.

Then add balsamic vinegar, mustard powder, sea salt, garlic powder, stir well for 2-3 minutes on high heat or fried well. When brussels sprouts are fried, add pomegranate and maple syrup, toss with brussels sprouts and pecans. Place them in a plate, spread pomegranate seeds over the plate. Decorate with fresh mint leaves.

Bon Appetit

MAPLE FRIED

BRUSSELS SPROUTS

ZUCCHINI, BELUGA, APPLE SALAD WITH

INGREDIENTS

Zucchini	2 MEDIUM
Carrot	1 MEDIUM
Red Apple	1 MEDIUM
Beetroot	1 SMALL
Cherry Tomatoes	A HANDFUL
Cilantro Leaves	1/4 BUNCH
Lemon Juice	4 TBSP
Beluga Lentils	2 TBSP
Peanuts	A HANDFUL

STAGE 1

Cut zucchinis spiral, cut carrot, apple and beet very thinly using a mandolin cutter. Cook beluga lentils for about 15 minutes. Strain and let it cool.

STAGE 2

Mix and place thinly cutted vegetables into the plate. Spread peanuts and beluga lentils. Decorate with cilantro. **Serve with tahini sauce and lemon.**

TAHINI SAUCE

2 TBSP Tahini,
1 TBSP Lemon Juice
1 TBSP Maple Syrup
1/8 TSP Salt
1/8 TSP Garlic Powder
Water to Thin

In a small bowl mix tahini sauce ingredients well. Pour over the salad.

Bon Appetit

TAHINI
D R E S S I N G

TIME
20 MINS

SERVING
2-3

DIFFUCULTY
10 / 3

ROASTED SUNCHOKES

The nutty sweetness of sunchokes most immediately lends itself to soft purées and soups, but they're more versatile than meets their knobby eyes.

INGREDIENTS

Sunchokes	400 GR	
Olive Oil	1 TBSP	
Tamari	1 TBSP	
Bay Leaves dried	2 LEAVES	
Thyme	1 TSP	
Garlic Powder	1 TSP	
Ground Mustard	1 TSP	
Pepper & Salt	TO TASTE	
Maple Syrup	1 TBSP	
Asparagus	3-4	
Fresh Dill chopped	2 TBSP	

STAGE 1

Wash and drain sunchokes. Divide them into two or three depending on their size.

STAGE 2

Pre-heat oven to 200 degrees. Mix olive oil, garlic, thyme, mustard, tamari, maple syrup, pepper and salt in a large bowl. Place sunchokes and asparagus in a bowl, toss with sauce.

STAGE 3

Lightly oil the baking sheet and place in the baking pan. Transfer sunchokes and asparagus into the pan. Roast for 25-30 minutes Decorate with chopped dill. Serve warm! Serve with spinach leaves, avocado slices if desired.

Serve warm!

Bon Appetit

WITH
S P I N A C H

TIME
40 MINS

SERVING
2-3

DIFFUCULTY
10 / 3

MAIN DISHES

FROM SIDE DISH TO STAR ATTRACTION, NO MENU IS COMPLETE WITHOUT A SALAD

Whether you're looking for hearty main dish salad recipes or light, nutritious fare, these salads are far from ordinary.

BUTTERNUT

RED LENTIL DAHL

This smooth red lentil Dahl melts in your mouth and will leave you coming back for more. An easy homemade curry recipe that is super simple, quick and comforting, quite like a hug on a mid-week night!

RED LENTIL DAHL

INGREDIENTS ———

Red Lentil	1 CUP
Garlic crushed	1 CLOVES
Red Onion	1 MEDIUM
Ground Ginger	1 TSP
Butternut Squash	100 GR
Coconut Milk	1/2 CUP
Curry Powder	1 TSP
Mushroom or Vegstock	1 CUP
Tamari	1 TBSP
Cayenne	1/2 TSP
Ground Coriander	1 TSP
Broccoli Florets	1 HEAD
Cherry Tomato	1 CUP

METHOD
POT

TIME
45 MINUTE

SERVING
3 PERSON

DIFFUCULTY
10/4

IT'S AN INDIAN STYLE RED LENTIL CURRY. IT CAN BE MADE MANY DIFFERENT WAYS, BUT I BELIEVE USING RED LENTILS IS THE MOST TRADITIONAL WAY. IT'S A MIX OF SLOWLY COOKED LENTILS WITH CURRY STYLE SPICES AND FINISHED WITH A DRIZZLE OF SPICY OIL DRIZZLED OVER TOP.

Indian style

DIRECTIONS

STEP I

Heat oil in a saucepan over a medium heat. Cook onions for 5-6 minutes until tender. Add garlic and curry powder. Cook for 2 minutes or until fragrant.

STEP II

Add lentils, butternut cubes, ginger, coriander, coconut milk, cayenne, salt and stock. Bring to the boil. Reduce heat to low. Simmer, partially covered, for 30 minutes or until lentils have softened. Cook, uncovered, stirring occasionally, for 20 to 30 minutes or until thickened. Remove from heat.

STEP III

In a large skillet pan, heat olive oil and tamari, add broccoli florets and occasionally stirring, cook broccoli on high heat until fried. Place red lentil dahl into a plate, add broccoli and cherry tomatoes. Serve warm with rice and lemon if desired.

Bon Appetit

CREAMY COCONUT CURRY

Sometimes I really don't feel like spending a lot of time making dinner, I just want to relax and do something else (although most of the time I still end up in the kitchen because, honestly i really love food) This recipe is also perfect for if you are short on time but still want to take a delicious meal to work. This sauce takes me less then 10 minutes to make and can be stored in the fridge for later use.

INGREDIENTS

Coconut Milk	230 ML
Olive Oil	1 TBSP
Garlic Puree	1 TSP
Ginger Powder	1/4 TSP
Worcestershire or Soy sauce	2 TBSP
Carrot julienne sliced	50 GR
Incaberries	6-7
Curry Powder	1 TSP
Shiitake or Porcini	100 GR
Nutritional Yeast	1 TBSP
Vegstock	100 ML
Lemon Juice	1 TBSP
Red Pepper Flakes	1 TSP

DIRECTIONS

1. In a large pot, add olive oil and chopped mushrooms and garlic. Cook on high heat for 5-6 minutes or until crispy.

2.Then add coconut cream, curry, ginger powder, vegan worchestershire sauce, incaberries halved, carrots, lemon juice, vegstock, nutritional yeast and pepper. Cook on medium heat for about 15 minutes or until thicken.

3. Transfer your cooked pasta into pan, toss with sauce.

4. Garnish with incaberries, vegan parmesan and thyme if desired. Serve warm.

Bon Appetit

COCONUT CURRY

F A R F E L L E

TIME

20 MINUTE

SERVING

3 PERSON

DIFFUCULTY

10 / 3

| **METHOD** | **TIME** | **SERVING** |
| POT | 25 MINUTE | 2 PERSON |

Green Lentil	1 CUP
Cherry Tomato	1 CUP
Avocado	1 RIPE
Garlic Granule	1 TSP
Salt	1 TSP
Cornstarch	2 TSP
Ground Mustard	1 TSP
Chili Flakes	1/2 TSP
Oat Cream (page 103)	250 GR
Sesame & Microgreens	TO DECORATE

GREEN & AWAKE

SIMPLE

IS THE BEST

A quick and easy recipe for savory oats and lentils that offers infinite variations and ... something smooth and creamy with avocado and tomatoes...

DIRECTIONS

STEP I

Wash and strain lentils, place in a pot, cover with filtered water. Cook for about 15-17 minutes or until soften.

STEP II

Place oat cream into the pot, add 1 teaspoon cornstarch, whisk well. Cook on medium heat until bubbled, then add garlic, salt, chili flakes, ground mustard, mix well. Add cooked lentils into the oat cream, stirring occasionally cook until tender.

STEP III

Place lentil in a large plate, add sliced avocado and cherry tomatoes. Add 1 tablespoon lemon juice over the avocado. Sprinkle salt. Decorate with celery micro greens, black and white sesame seeds.

Bon Appetit

OAT CREAM

HOW TO MAKE?

1/2 CUP ROLLED OATS

1 CUP WATER

1 TBSP MAPLE SYRUP

2 TSP TAPIOCA STARCH

3 TBSP MELTED COCONUT OIL

1 TSP HIMALAYAN SALT

Soak the oats in the water overnight, then in the morning blend in a food processor with the maple syrup, salt and the tapioca starch. With the food processor running slowly add the melted coconut oil, process until combined and silky smooth. Chill in the fridge until thickened. Heat in the pot before using.

"Easy and versatile, this cream is great with cooked legumes"

GRILLED TOFU

WITH HABANERO & NOODLE

GRILLED TOFU HABANERO

INGREDIENTS

Firm Tofu	250 GR
Lemon Juice	2 TBSP
Maple Syrup	1 TBSP
Soy Sauce	2 TBSP
Porcini or Veg Stock	1/4 CUP
Coconut Cream	150 ML
Garlic Powder	1 TSP
Chili Powder	1 TSP
Konjac Noodle	200 GR
Kale Leaves	100 GR
Olive Oil	1 TBSP
Sea Salt	1 TSP
Red Bell Pepper	2 LARGE
Cayenne	1/2 TSP

METHOD
OVEN

TIME
55 MINUTE

SERVING
2 PERSON

DIFFUCULTY
10/6

TO MAKE PORCINI MUSHROOM STOCK

ADD THE ONION, LEEK TOP, GARLIC, MUSHROOMS, AND SALT. GIVE THE VEGETABLES A STIR, THEN COVER THE POT AND COOK GENTLY OVER MEDIUM HEAT FOR 15 MINUTES. ADD THE REMAINING INGREDIENTS AND COVER WITH 9 CUPS COLD WATER. BRING THE STOCK TO A BOIL, THEN SIMMER, UNCOVERED, FOR 1 HOUR.

A good protein Source

DIRECTIONS

STEP I

In a large bowl, add mushroom stock, 1 tablespoon lemon juice, 2 tablespoons of soy sauce, 1 tablespoon maple syrup, garlic powder and chili pepper. Cut your tofu in desired shape and marinate in the sauce for about 1 hours. Roast chili peppers at 220 degrees in the oven for about 22-25 minutes. Peel and remove the skin.

STEP II

Place roasted chili into the food processor, add coconut cream, 1 tablespoon lemon juice, shoyu, cayenne pepper, paprika and salt. Mix on high speed until smooth. Then transfer mixture into a pot and cook on medium heat until bubbled.

STEP III

Strain your konjac noodle, set aside. In a large skillet, heat 1 tablespoon olive oil, add kale leaves and sprinkle a bit salt. Stir-fry on high heat for 1-2 minutes. Then add konjac noodle, toss with kale leaves. Grill your marinated tofu until fried well. Pour chili coconut sauce into your plate, add grilled tofu onto the sauce. Add konjac noodle with kale. Sprinkle some sesame. Serve warm!

Bon Appetit

COUSCOUS

WITH CARROTS AND CASHEWS

Spicy and fresh, this recipe works well on its own as a delicious cold salad for a light yet filling meal, or served warm as a side dish.

SPICY COUSCOUS

INGREDIENTS ———

Purple Orange Carrots	2-3
Olive Oil	2 TBSP
Paprika	1 TSP
Turmeric	1 TSP
Mustard Sauce	1 TSP
Rosemary Chopped	1 TSP
Smoked Paprika	1/2 TSP

TIME
40 MINUTE

SERVING
2 PERSON

DIFFUCULTY
10/3

Giant Couscous	1 CUP
Cashew Nuts	30 GR
Parsley	1/2 BUNCH
Sea Salt	TO TASTE

DIRECTIONS

STEP I

Pre-heat the oven to 220 degrees. Peel and chop the carrots, place in a roasting pan and toss with 1 tablespoon of oil, ground mustard and garlic powder. Spread out in an even layer and roast in the oven at least 20 minutes.

STEP II

Wash and strain couscous, cover with water and cook for 10-15 minutes. Drain and set aside to cool. Place the cashew nuts in a pan and cook them over medium heat for a few minutes until golden brown. Make sure you stir often as they can burn easily.

STEP III

Mix carrots, couscous, chopped parsley and the cashews together and dress with the remaining tablespoon of olive oil, other herbs, mustard sauce and lemon juice. Serve warm!

Bon Appetit

METHOD

OVEN

TIME

25 MINUTE

SERVING

4 PERSON

Potatoes	300 GR	
Brussels Sprouts	200 GR	
Olive Oil	2 TBSP	
Garlic Powder	1 TSP	
Almond Milk	2 TBSP	
Sea Salt	1 TSP	
Black Pepper	1/4 TSP	

GREEN & AWAKE

COMFORT

F O O D

Comfort food is a staple for anyone wanting a hearty meals and a little taste of home. Enjoy by starting to mash potatoes and top with oven baked brussels sprouts, serve with avocado pesto!

DIRECTIONS

STEP I

Wash, drain and cut brussels sprouts in half. Drizzle with olive oil and bake in the oven at 200 degrees until fried.

STEP II

Place the potatoes in a large pot, cover with cold water. Add a little salt in to the water. Over high heat, bring the water to a boil, then reduce heat to maintain a low boil. Cook for about 25-30 minutes or until potatoes are very tender.

STEP III

Drain potatoes well and remove the skin. Place them in a food processor, add almond milk, salt & pepper. Mix on high speed until smooth and creamy. Add an additional tablespoons of almond milk if you need. But be careful, because too much milk can make the potatoes soupy. ransfer potatoes into a bowl, add baked brussels sprouts on top.

Bon Appetit

AVOCADO PESTO

&

BRUSSELS SPROUTS

———————

PROVENCE HERBS TO TASTE

1 RIPE AVOCADO

1 TBSP LEMON JUICE

1/2 CUP FRESH BASIL

A HANDFUL OF RAW WALNUTS

Place fresh basil, lemon juice, salt, avocado and walnut into the food processor, mix on high speed until smooth.

ransfer in a small bowl. Serve with mashed potatoes and baked brussel sprouts

METHOD
POT

TIME
15 MINUTE

SERVING
2 PERSON

Firm Tofu	150 GR
Peanut Butter	3 TBSP
Ginger Chopped	1 SMALL
Apple Vinegar	1 TBSP
Soy Sauce	2 TBSP
Cucumber	1 MEDIUM
Green Apple	1 SMALL
Agave Syrup	1 TBSP
Sesame	1 TSP
Mint & Green Onion	TO DECORATE

PROTEIN
SOURCE

If you don't feel like cooking on a hot summer day, you can enjoy plain cold tofu with a dipping sauce or you can sear it quickly in a pan or grill it.

DIRECTIONS

STEP I

Wash the tofu, cut it into small cubes. Drizzle with olive oil and fry each face of tofu cubes in a skillet pan on high heat. Wash apples and cut into cubes. ry them in a pan, pour over agave syrup and sesame and mix them, then transfer on a paper towel to absorb oil.

STEP II

Cut cucumbers and place them at the bottom of the serving tray. Add fried apples, toss together.
Wash and peel ginger. place in a blender, mix on high speed until chopped. If it is very grainy, you can filter it with the help of a cheesecloth.

STEP III

Mix peanut butter in a bowl, 5 tablespoons of warm water, soy sauce, apple juice and chopped ginger.
Add the tofu into the bowl and mix them.
Place the remaining apple cubes on top of the tofu cubes and put a few more tofu and sauce on the bottom of the bowl.
Sprinkle onion and mint leaves.

Bon Appetit

TOFU GUIDE

The Difference Between Types of Fresh Tofu

Regular tofu is pressed and has a somewhat spongy texture, and comes in several varieties distinguished by how much water is pressed out. Soft tofu has the least amount of water pressed out, while super-firm has a low moisture content and a dense texture. Silken tofu works well in creamy and blended foods like smoothies, desserts, puddings, salad dressings, sauces, and dips. It can also be used as an egg substitute in baking

Soft tofu is the Chinese-style equivalent of silken tofu. It is slightly less smooth but can be used in the same way as silken tofu. Medium tofu is denser than silken and soft but still fairly delicate. It can work well in gently simmered soups like miso and served cold like hiya yakko. Depending on the brand, it may be interchangeable with firm tofu. Firm tofu absorbs flavors well and can be stir-fried and pan-fried (how well it will hold together depends on the brand). It's also great crumbled and used in tofu scramble and as a substitute for ricotta cheese

CREAMY PUMPKIN

PIPETTE

CREAMY PUMPKIN PIPETTE

INGREDIENTS ——————

Pipette Pasta	250 GR
Butternut Squash	300 GR
Shallot	4-5
Olive Oil	1 TBSP
Salt	2 TSP
Ground Mustard	1 TSP
Pine Nuts	25 GR
Fresh Rosemary	1 TBSP
Nutritional Yeast	1 TBSP
Water	TO THIN
Garlic Powder	1 TSP
Sesame Seeds	1 TBSP
Cherry Tomato	7-8

METHOD POT

TIME 45 MINUTE

SERVING 3 PERSON

DIFFUCULTY 10/4

THE KEY TO BALANCING THE RICHNESS OF THE CREAM AND THE SWEETNESS OF THE PUMPKIN IN THIS SIMPLE SAUCE IS SALTY, STARCHY PASTA WATER.

DIRECTIONS

STEP I

Cook your pasta al dente, strain and set aside. Cut butternut squash into cubes, place into a bowl. ut shallots in two, add to bowl. Add salt, olive oil, mustard, nutritional yeast, garlic and rosemary. Mix with your hands well. And transfer mixture into baking tray with parchment paper.

STEP II

Pre-heat oven to 200 degrees. Bake mixture in the oven for about 22-25 minutes or until roasted. Remove roasted butternut squash from the oven, place in a food processor, add 1/2 cup water. Mix on high speed until smooth. If you need, add more water to thin.

STEP III

Pour sauce into the pot. Cook on medium heat until bubbled. hen add your cooked pipette pasta and mix with sauce. Serve with cherry tomatoes, roasted pine nuts, celery micro greens and sesame seeds.

Bon Appetit

PORCINI SWISS CHARD

TIME
1 HOUR

SERVING
3 PERSON

DIFFUCULTY
10 / 3

festive

INGREDIENTS

Porcini Mushrooms	70	GR
Grapeseed Oil	2	TBSP
Shoyu	2	TBSP
Garlic Powder	1	TSP
Fresh Cilantro	2	TBSP
Purple Potatoes	250	GR
Yukon Gold Potatoes	50	GR
Beluga Lentil	70	GR
Swiss Chard Leaves	6-7	LARGE
Sesame Seeds	1	TBSP
Sea Salt	1	TSP

Tahini	4	TBSP
Minced Ginger	1	TSP
Shoyu	2	TBSP
Lemon Juice	2	TBSP
Maple Syrup	2	TBSP
Garlic Cloves	1	CRUSHED
Habanero	1	TSP
Spring Water	2	TBSP

DIRECTIONS

Brush, wash and drain your mushrooms, if you will use fried mushrooms, then soak them in warm water at least 15 minutes and strain. Set aside.

In a large skillet, heat grapeseed oil, add shoyu and garlic powder. Transfer mushrooms into the skillet, cook until fried.
Bake cutted potatoes at 220 degrees for about 25-30 minutes. Heat a bit olive oil in a large pan, add swiss chards, sprinkle salt.
Cook on high heat for 1-2 minutes. Wash and strain beluga lentils.
Cover with water and cook for 20 minutes. Place swiss chards into a bowl, add fried potatoes, mushrooms and lentils. Place all sauce ingredients into a blender, mix until smooth.
Use more or less water to achieve desired consistency. Pour mixture over the bowl.
Decorate with sesame seeds and cilantro. Serve warm.

Bon Appetit

PORCINI SWISS CHARD

POTATO & BELUGA WITH GINGER

AN ELEGANT
DISH

METHOD	TIME	SERVING
POT	55 MINUTE	6-8

Fresh Zucchini Blossoms	20-22
White Quinoa	1 CUP
Mango	1 RIPE
Fresh Dill, Parsley, Mint	A HANDFUL
Salt	1 TSP
Garlic Chopped	1 CLOVE
Onion Chopped	1 SMALL
Walnut Oil	6 TBSP
Lemon Juice	1
Red & Green Pepper	2 SMALL

Sprinkle a pinch of basil or dill. Pour 2 tbsp walnut oil before serving..

DIRECTIONS

STEP I

Soak the zucchini flowers in a large bowl of cold water and wash very well. Set aside. Wash the quinoa and cook with 1/2 cup warm water for about 2 - 3 minutes. Set aside.

STEP II

Combine 2 tbsp walnut oil, chopped onions, minced garlic, salt, chopped peppers, dill, parsley and mint in a pan. Stir until they are soften. Then add the quinoa and 50ml. warm water. Cook mixture for about 4-5 minutes. Fill each flower with the mixture using a small teaspoon and squeeze gently to firm up.

STEP III

Place stuffed zucchini blossoms in a pan and add warm water until just over level with the top of them. Add 2 tbsp olive oil, coconut sugar and lime juice. Bring to boil on medium heat for 20 minutes or cook until quinoa is fluffy and blossoms are tender. Roast the blossoms in the oven at 200 degrees for 15 minutes or until they are fried.

Bon Appetit

QUINOA STUFFED
ZUCCHINI BLOSSOM

This stuffed zucchini blossoms recipe makes a delightful appetizer, and they are often stuffed with mixtures similar to fillings used in stuffed leaves and vegetables.

The pistil and stamen do not need to be removed, but most Greek cooks do take them out. Blossoms can be used from winter and summer squash. If picking your own fresh blossoms pick early in the morning while blossoms are open. Separate from the stalk,

METHOD
POT

TIME
35 MINUTE

SERVING
2 PERSON

Penne	300 GR
Fresh Basil	100 GR
Oat Milk	1/2 CUP
Walnut or Pine Nuts	100 GR
Salt	1/2 TSP
Olive Oil	100 ML
Nutritional Yeast	2 TBSP
Cherry Tomatoes	1 CUP
Vegan Parmesan	2 TBSP
Sesame & Microgreens	TO DECORATE

ITALIAN
TASTE

A quick and easy recipe for savory oats that offers infinite variations and ... something smooth and creamy with avocado and tomatoes...

GREEN & AWAKE

DIRECTIONS

STEP I

In a large pot, place penne, cover with warm water, add a bit olive oil and salt. Bring to boil until al dente. Strain your penne, set aside.

STEP II

Wash and drain basil leaves. Place into the food processor. Add oat milk, salt, pine nuts, olive oil and nutritional yeast. Mix on high speed until completely smooth. Pour mixture into the pot. Cook on low heat occasionally stirring for about 4-5 minutes.

STEP III

Add cooked penne into the pot. Toss with sauce.
Divide cherry tomatoes in two, spread over the pasta.
Sprinkle sesame seeds and microgreens.
You can also add extra pine nuts before serving. For this in a small pan, heat olive oil, fry nuts on medium heat for about 2-3 minutes.

Bon Appetit

PESTO ALLA

GENOVESE

Pesto is a sauce originating in Genoa, which is located in the northern region of Italy. It originated around the 16th century and traditionally consists of crushed garlic,
basil and pine nuts blended with Parmesan and olive oil. In this recipe I veganized it
and made more creamy consistency with oat milk.

Enjoy!

A restaurant quality dish, only takes 22 minutes!

JACK IN WONDERLAND

INGREDIENTS ——

Onion Chopped	1 MEDIUM
Olive Oil	4 TBSP
Artichoke Hearts	200 GR
Jack Fruit	400 GR
Garlic Powder	1 TSP
Coconut Sugar	1 TBSP
Chili Pepper	1 TSP
Thyme	1 TSP
Apple Cider Vinegar	1/2 TBSP
Ground Mustard	1 TSP
Sea Salt	1 TSP
Vegan Worcestershire	3 TBSP
Tomato Paste	1 TBSP
Lingonberry Jam	2 TBSP

DIRECTIONS ———

1. Heat a large skillet with 3 tablespoon olive oil. Add sliced onions and sauté until caramelized.

2. Add sliced jack fruits, 1 tablespoon soy sauce and marinated artichoke hearts. Cook stirring occasionally for about 8-10 minutes on medium heat until softened and crispy.

3. In a small bow, mix garlic powder, coconut sugar, chili pepper, apple cider vinegar, thyme, mustard powder, sea salt, Worcestershire sauce, 1 tbsp olive oil and tomato paste.

4.Pour mixture over the jack fruit artichoke mixture. Toss well until jack and artichokes are coated well. Using a small spoon draw a round with lingonberry jam on the plate. Decorate with sesame seeds, thinly sliced radish, pickled red onion, edible flowers, if desired.

ROASTED SEITAN

METHOD
OVEN +POT

TIME
2H 50M

SERVING
8-10

WET INGREDIENTS

Vegetable Broth	1 LITER
Water	2 CUPS
Soy Sauce	5-6 TBSP
Olive Oil	3-4 TBSP
Beet Puree	80 GR
Shiitake Powder	2 TBSP
Worcestershire Sauce	3 TBSP
Blackpepper	A PINCH

DRY INGREDIENTS

Vital Gluten	2 CUPS
Chickpea Flour	1 CUP
Onion Powder	3 TBSP
Garlic Powder	2 TBSP

GLAZING

Vegan Butter	3 TBSP
Worcestershire	3 TBSP
Agave Syrup	1 TBSP
Water & Spices	2 TBSP & TO TASTE

STIR-FRY

Olive Oil	3-4 TBSP
Soy Sauce	4-5 TBSP

DIRECTIONS

STEP I

In a large bowl, combine all dry ingredients and set aside. Place all wet ingredients in a food processor, mix on high completely smooth. Add dry ingredients into the blender, mix well.

STEP II

Remove dough from the food processor, knead with your hands for 1-2 minutes. Give a bread shape. Pre-heat oven to 180 degrees. Place a baking sheet in a baking pan. Transfer dough on to the pan. Bake for 1 hour and 20 minutes. Using a large pot, bring the broth to boil.

STEP III

When the roast is finished, place it inside the pot. Monitor the pot frequently to make sure the broth is simmering, not boiling. Turn it continuously. Boil for 1 hour. Refrigerate the seitan overnight to get best texture.

GLAZING SAUCE

————————

To make glazing sauce, place all sauce ingredients in a small pot, cook for 3-4 minutes on medium heat. If you need add more water or agave syrup to get sticky sauce.
Next morning, spread sauce over the seitan. Let it cool at least 30 min. Cut into small long pieces or cubes. Heat stir fry ingredients; olive oil and soy sauce in large pan, add seitan pieces, stir-fry on high heat until crispy. Serve with your favorite greens and nuts.

Liquid tips:

to turn seitan into dark color, use more soy sauce and vegetable broth.

to make a soft texture, use only water.

to make spicy and intense seitan, use more soy sauce and peppers.

〜〜〜〜〜〜〜〜〜〜

Bon Appetit

SPINACH RAVIOLI

METHOD
POT

TIME
25 MINUTE

SERVING
4

DOUGH

Whole Wheat Flour (or buckwheat)	350	GR
Water	100	ML
Olive Oil	2	TBSP
Egg Replacer (Lupin Powder)	1	TSP
Water	70	ML
Sea Salt	1/2	TSP

FILLING

Leak	1	LONG
Olive Oil	2	TBSP
Garlic Cloves	2	
Red Pepper	1	LARGE
Spinach	200	GR
Vegan Parmesan	100	GR
Salt	1	TBSP

TOPPINGS

Vegan Parmesan

Sesame Seeds , Pine Nuts

Celery Microgreens

DIRECTIONS

STEP I

In a small bowl, mix egg replacer (I use Arche VegEgg brand) and 70 ml water well. Set aside. To make dough, place all dough ingredients in a large bowl, add egg replacer mixture and mix dough with your hands until it forms shaggy mass. If you need , add more flour or water. Cover dough with a plastic wrap and let it rest for 10-15 minutes.

STEP II

To prepare filling, mix chopped leeks and peppers with olive oil in a pan until caramelized. Then add spinach, garlic, salt and peppers. Stir and cook on medium heat for 3-4 minutes. Add vegan parmesan into the pan, mix and set aside.

STEP III

Cut dough into 2 pieces.
Roll each piece out very thinly while using a rolling pin.
Dust the ravioli mold with flour.
Lay one piece of dough over the ravioli mold and put a 1/2 tsp of filling into each ravioli. Lay second piece of dough over the top.

STEP IV

Pinch the edges together and then seal the edges of the ravioli with a fork or your hands. Make sure to press firmly and go all the way around. Repeat this process for all your dough pieces. Bring to boil them in warm water for 4-5 minutes. Strain and place into the plate. Drizzle with olive oil.

Grate vegan parmesan if desired, top with pine nuts, sesame and micro greens.

Bon Appetit

CREAMY CHICKPEAS CURRY

OVEN   50 MINS   2-3 PERSON   10/4

SALAD INGREDIENTS

Chanterelle Mushrooms	1	CUP
Cherry Tomato	1	TBSP
Red Bell Peppers	2	TBSP
Red Onion	1/2	TSP
Olive Oil	1	SMALL
Tamari	3-4	TBSP
Garlic	2	CLOVES
Coconut Milk	220	ML
Salt	1/2	TSP
Nutritional Yeast	3	TBSP
Rosemary	1/4	TSP
Lemon Juice	1/2	
Paprika	1/2	TSP
Chickpeas	1	CUP

STEP I
Pre-heat oven to 200 degrees.
Bake red peppers for about 25-30 minutes.
Then remove skin and seeds. Set aside. Place
chickpeas in a pot, cover with water. Bring to
boil until soften.

STEP II
**Heat up a large skillet pan, sauce onion
and garlic in olive oil until golden brown.
Set aside.**
Place coconut milk, red peppers, nutritional
yeast, cornstarch, salt and smoked paprika in
to the food processor. Mix on high speed until combined well.

WITH CHANTERELLE

STEP III

Heat up a large skillet pan, add chanterelle mushrooms, add 1 tablespoon olive oil, lemon juice, rosemary, and tamari. Saute on high heat until golden brown. Then add cooked chickpeas, cook one more minute by occasionally stirring.

Cut tomatoes in half and add to the pan. Cook for about 1-2 minutes on high heat with mushrooms.

Then add sauted onion garlic mixture and coconut curry sauce into the pan. Stir well.

Transfer food in a large bowl.

Bake in the oven for about 15-20 minutes. Serve with rice warm!

Bon Appetit

BUCKOTTO

WITH MUSHROOMS

BUCKOTTO

INGREDIENTS ———

Mushrooms	400 GR
Raw Buckwheat	100 GR
Water	100 ML
Onion Chopped	1 MEDIUM
Garlic Powder	1 TSP
Soy Sauce	1 TBSP
Oat Cream	125 ML
Olive Oil	2 TBSP
Red & Green Pepper	2 LARGE
Tarragon Leaves	TO DECORATE
Sesame Seeds	1 TSP
Salt	1 TSP

METHOD
POT

TIME
40 MINS

SERVING
3-4

DIFFICULTY
10/4

THIS IS A NEW VERSION OF CLASSIC RISOTTO. MADE WITH BUCK-WHEATS, OAT CREAM AND MUSHROOMS.

Buckwheat Risotto

DIRECTIONS

STEP I

Brush mushrooms and slice them in thin slices. Cut peppers into small pieces. In a large skillet add olive oil, peppers and onion. Stir fry on high heat for 2 minutes.

STEP II

Then add mushroom slices, soy sauce, thyme, salt and garlic powder. Cook on medium heat until browned and tendered. Add oat cream and cook for 5 minutes.

STEP III

In a small pot, place buckwheats. Cover with water and bring to boil for 20 minutes or until lightly soften. Then remove, strain and transfer them into the skillet. Mix with mushrooms well. Decorate with parsley or your favorite herbs.

Bon Appetit

CHIPOTLE BLACK BEANS

SIMPLE, CONVENIENT AND DELICIOUS

TIME	SERVING	DIFFICULTY
1 HOUR	3 PERSON	10 / 3

Savory

INGREDIENTS

Black Beans	200	GR
Olive Oil	1	TBSP
Leek	1	MEDIUM
Carrot	1	MEDIUM
Potato	2	SMALL
jalapeno	1	MEDIUM
Vegetable Cube	1	CUBE
Nutritional Yeast	1/2	TBSP
Salt	1	TSP
Garlic	1	TSP
Ground Mustard	1/2	TSP
Tomato Paste	1	TBSP
Cherry Tomatoes	175	GR
Chipotle Powder	1	TSP

CHIPOTLE ACTUALLY IS NOTHING MORE THAN JALAPENO PEPPER THAT HAS BEEN SMOKED AND DRIED. TYPICALLY, IT IS THEN GROUND INTO A SPICE,

PROVIDING THE SMOKY FLAVOR THAT YOU ARE LIKELY ACCUSTOMED TO WHEN HAVING A CHIPOTLE-BASED DISH.

DIRECTIONS

Wash beans, place in a deep pot, cover with water. Bring to boil until lightly soft. Strain and set aside.

In a large pan, heat olive oil, add chopped leeks, carrots, potatoes, jalapeno. Saute until caramelized. Then add, cherry tomatoes, garlic, mustard, tomato paste chili powder, salt and nutritional yeast. Stir and add 200ml. water. Cook on medium heat for 5 minutes. Then add vegetable cube, chipotle spice, beans and cook until lightly softened. Cook on medium heat for 10 minutes. Pre-heat oven to 200 degrees. Transfer meal into the dutch oven. Roast for 15-20 minutes or until golden browned. Let it cool for 15 minutes before serving. Top with fresh mint leaves or parsley if desired.

Bon Appetit

CHIPOTLE

BLACK BEANS

TEMPEH WITH CELERY SAUCE

METHOD
POT

TIME
50 MINUTE

SERVING
4

TEMPEH INGREDIENTS

Dry Chickpeas	1 CUP
White Vinegar	1 TBSP
Tempeh Starter	1 TSP

DIRECTIONS

1. Place the chickpeas in a large bowl, cover with clean water soak for 8 hours or overnight.

2. The next day, drain and rinse the chickpeas. Transfer to a large cooking pot, cover with water (about 2-inch higher than the chickpeas). Bring to a boil and let simmer for 1 hour. Depending on the size of your chickpeas it might take up to 1 and 1/2 hour. They must be soft but not mushy. If some foam forms on the surface during cooking, remove it with a spoon to prevent any spillover.

3. Once the chickpeas are cooked, drain them and leave them in the strainer for 30 minutes. After that, pat them dry using a paper towel to make sure they are mostly dry on the outside. Transfer to a large clean bowl. Add the white vinegar and stir to coat. Add the tempeh starter and mix well using a spoon until uniformly distributed. Using a metal skewer, or chopstick, prick some holes (at about 2-inch intervals) in a clean freezer bag. This step is important to create good air circulation and allow the mold to grow.

4. Transfer the chickpeas to the freezer bag and form a rectangle of about 5×8 inches with a thickness of about 1-inch. Place the bag of chickpeas on a baking sheet and put in an oven with the light on for about 14 hours. I set the temperature of my oven to 86°F and let the door very slightly opened because I can't just let the light on.

5. After 14 hours, some white mold (not a lot) should have appeared on the chickpeas. You might also see some condensation inside the plastic bag, this is normal. It's time to remove the baking sheet from the oven and let it ferment for another 24-36H in a dark and warm place. I recommend covering the chickpea bag with a clean towel to make sure it's not under direct sunlight.

6. Your tempeh is ready when it is fully covered with white mold and forms a solid cake, which usually happens at the 48-hour mark. It can be quicker if the temperature in your house is high.

Raw tempeh will keep for up to a week in the refrigerator. If you want to freeze it: steam the tempeh for 25 minutes, let cool completely and wrap in plastic film before freezing.

CELERIAC PUREE

1 large celeriac, peeled and diced
(about 2 heaping cups),
1 tablespoon olive oil,
1 large red onion chopped,
2 garlic cloves- rough chopped,
1 cup water,
1/4 teaspoon salt
1/4 teaspoon white pepper

CELERY GRAMOLATA

2 cups of celery leaves and stems,
1/2 cup olive oil,
1-2 garlic cloves,
Zest of one meyer lemon, plus 1-2
teaspoons lemon juice,
1/2 cup salt and white pepper

D I R E C T I O N S

─────────────

1.Preheat oven to 180 C, in a small bowl olive oil, garlic, pepper, lemon zest and salt. Brush all sides of the tempeh with the marinade and liberally coat the top -place on parchment paper. Place in the oven for 30 minutes or until golden.While the it is baking make the Celeriac Puree.

2. Peel the celeriac using a sharp paring knife and dice. Heat oil over medium heat in a large skillet and saute the onion and garlic until golden and fragrant, about 2-3 minutes. Add the celeriac and water. Bring to a simmer, cover and simmer gently for 10 minutes or until fork tender. When tender, add the celeriac and any remaining liquid into the blendtec. Blend until smooth, add salt, pepper and more water to get a silky smooth consistency.

3.Divide the Celeriac Puree among two bowls, top with the tempehand spoon a little Gremolata over top.

To make Celery Gremolata: place all gremolata ingredients into the food processor. Mix on high speed until smooth. Store in a jar in the fridge for up to 1 week.

Enjoy!

WILTED SWISS CHARD & LENTILS

TIME
1 HOUR

SERVING
3 PERSON

DIFFICULTY
10 / 4

INGREDIENTS

3-4 small beets,

7-8 large swiss chard leaves,

250 gr. sunchokes,

1 cup cooked green lentil,

2 tbsp olive oil,

1 large red onion diced,

2 garlic cloves minced,

1-2 tbsp balsamic vinegar,

4-5 tbsp vegan parmesan (optional),

Fresh thyme,

Salt and blackpepper to taste

A SIMPLE HEARTY MEAL THAT IS NOT ONLY FILLING– IT IT IS HEALTHY AND DELICIOUS TOO.

SWISS CHARDS ARE BRIGHTENING LENTILS UP, AND BRINGING OUT THE BEST IN THEM. IT'S A GOOD MARRIAGE WITH ROASTED BEETS AND SUNCHOKES AS WELL.
ENJOY!

DIRECTIONS

1. Preheat oven to 200 C. Scrub and trim beets and sunchokes and cut into ½ inch slices or wedges. Place on a foil lined baking sheet. Drizzle with olive oil and roast until tender, about 30 minutes.

2. To cook lentils, place green lentils in a small pot and cover with 3 inches of water and a pinch salt. Bring to a boil, cover and turn heat down to a simmer, cook until tender (it usually takes 20 minutes, should still hold their shape.) Then Drain.

3. In a large skillet, heat 2 tablespoons oil over medium high heat. Add diced onion and saute 3-4 minutes. Turn heat down to medium, add garlic and cook 2 more minutes, until golden and fragrant.

4. Lower heat to medium low. Add chard and gently wilt, just slightly, about 2-3 more minutes. Season with salt and pepper.

5.Add cooked lentils to the skillet, gently folding them in and warming.

6. Add beets and sunchokes then splash with 1-2 tablespoons balsamic vinegar. Let vinegar cook down for just a couple minutes so it's not so acidic. Sprinkle with vegan parmesan and fresh thyme.
Taste again, if it tastes bland it most likely needs salt. Serve immediately.

WILTED SWISS CHARD & LENTILS

WITH ROASTED BEETS & SUNCHOKES

BROCCOLI PENNE

MEET THE CREAMIEST VEGAN ALFREDO SAUCE,
MADE WITH OAT AND LOTS OF GARLIC!

TIME
20 MINS

SERVING
2 PERSON

DIFFICULTY
10 / 3

INGREDIENTS

Ingredient	Amount	
Vegan Butter	3	TBSP
Flour	3	TBSP
Oat Milk	2	CUPS
Nutritional Yeast	3	TBSP
Penne	250	GR
Garlic Powder	1/2	TSP
Onion Powder	1/4	TSP
Salt	1	TSP
Tamari	2	TBSP
Olive Oil	2	TBSP
Broccoli Florets	2	CUPS
Salt and Pepper		TO TASTE

MAKE YOUR OWN OAT MILK

Soak 1 cup oats in purified water for at least 30 minutes, After soaking, drain and rinse the oats well. Put soaked, rinsed, drained oats into blender, add 3 cups of purified water. Blend and strain in a nut milk bag to remove pulp.

DIRECTIONS

In a medium pan, heat oil on medium heat. Add flour slowly. Cook for 1-2 minutes, continue to whisk until smooth. Then add oat milk, salt, garlic, onion powder and nutritional yeast. Turn heat to medium-low and cook until thicken.

Cook your pasta according to package and set aside. Heat a larg skillet pan, add olive oil and tamari. Stir-fry broccoli florets on high heat for 2-3 minutes.
Transfer broccoli florets into the sauce.
Add pasta into the pot. Mix well together. Serve warm.

ALFREDO

BROCCOLI PENNE

PINK SPAGHETTI

VODKA ROASTED BEET & ALMOND

INGREDIENTS ———

Beetroot	250 GR
Vodka	3 TBSP
Almond Flour	2 TBSP
Onion Powder	1/2 TSP
Almond Milk	1/2 CUP
Garlic Powder	1/2 TSP
Black pepper	A PINCH
Sea Salt	1 TSP
Olive Oil	2 TBSP
Vegan Parmesan	50 GR
Spaghetti	250 GR
Oregano	A PINCH
Onion Chives	TO DECORATE

METHOD	TIME	SERVING	DIFFICULTY
POT	35 MINS	2	10/4

THIS ROMANTIC RECIPE FOR BEET PASTA WITH ALMOND AND VODKA IS ALMOST AS ENJOYABLE TO MAKE AS IT IS TO EAT!

A simple gourmet dish

DIRECTIONS

STEP I

Bring to boil beets on high heat for 15 minutes.
Pre-heat oven to 200 degrees. Then put beets into a pyrex, pour 2 tbsp vodka and 1 tbsp olive oil over the beet and cook in the oven for 20 minutes

STEP II

Place roasted beets, almond meal, almond milk, garlic, onion, pepper and salt in a food processor, mix on high until get completely smooth mixture.

STEP III

Transfer mixture in a large pan, add 1 tbsp olive oil, stir on medium heat for 5-6 minutes. Add spaghetti into the sauce. Mix until well combined. Garnish oregano or oniin chives. Serve warm with vegan parmesan.

Bon Appetit

CABBAGE WITH BLACK RICE, QUINOA AND MUSTARD

METHOD
POT

TIME
25 MINUTE

SERVING
4

THE BLACK RICE IS NUTTY AND SEMI-SWEET. IT PAIRS WELL WITH ANYTHING! BUT BEST WITH STIR-FRY CABBAGE AND PARSLEY.

INGREDIENTS

1 bunch collard greens or kale chopped thinly

250 gr. brussels sprouts shredded

250 gr. white cabbage shredded

3-4 tbsp hemp hearts

1/2 cup black wild rice cooked

1/2 cup quinoa cooked (optional)

DRESSING

5 tbsp lemon juice

2 tbsp mustard

1 tbsp maple syrup

1/2 tsp salt

2 tbsp olive oil

1/2 bunch fresh parsley chopped

DIRECTIONS

1. Shave the brussels sprouts and cabbage using a sharp knife. Add them to a large bowl.

2. Thinly slice the kale into fine ribbons. I like to roll the kale leaves together width-wise and then slice them from top to bottom. It's quick and easy! Add these to the bowl as well.

3. You can eat them as raw by combining with the mustard dressing or wilt with stir-fry method.

4. In a separate small bowl, combine salt, mustard, lemon juice and olive oil. Whisk together to form the dressing. Pour the dressing over the ingredients in the bowl and massage together with your hands. Taste and adjust seasoning as needed.

5. Add cooked black rice and quinoa.

6. Serve with hemp hearts and fresh parsley. (Add some mashed avocado and lemon juice if you prefer, it goes so well with black rice and cabbage too)

Bon Appetit

WHITE CABBAGE

WITH BLACK RICE, QUINOA & MUSTARD

BAKING DESSERTS

ENJOY WITH MY SIGNATURE VEGANIZED SCANDINAVIAN TREATS

If dessert is your favourite part of the meal, then this collection is for you! Filled with luscious mousses, creamy chocolate and comforting fruit jam!

CHOCOLATE

W / HAZELNUT & QUINOA

C H O C O L A T E

I N G R E D I E N T S

Cacao Butter	60 GR
Coconut Oil	50 GR
Vanilla Extract	1 TSP
Hazelnut or Almond	A HANDFUL
Cacao Mass	50 GR
Agave Syrup	50 GR
Dried Mulberries	A HANDFUL

METHOD
POT

TIME
25 MINUTE

SERVING
3-4

DIFFICULTY
10/6

TIP: FOR A STRONGER CHOCOLATE FLAVOR, USE 2 OUNCES (60G) OF COCOA POWDER

Nothing Beats Homemade

D I R E C T I O N S

STEP I

Melt cacao butter in a double boiler with the lowest heat setting. The temperature should be around 107°F (42°C) to keep it in raw. Add the cacao mass and mix until smooth. Once mixed, add the agave and mix again mix until completely liquid.

STEP II

Place an oily paper into the pyrex or pan. Pour chocolate.

STEP III

Spread crushed hazelnuts or sliced almonds , dried mulberries and quinoa pops. Let it rest at least 30 minutes in room temperature. Then Place into the refrigerator at least 3 hours before using. (This is a simple chocolate recipe, not tempered. Continue with " gourmet raw cakebook" to see how to temper raw chocolate" if you are interested.)

Bon Appetit

CRISPY CROISSANT

METHOD
POT

TIME
25 MINUTE

SERVING
6

NOTHING SAYS WEEKEND LIKE A WARM CROISSANT FROM THE OVEN.

PEOPLE OFTEN THINK OF FRANCE WHEN THEY HEAR MENTION OF THE CROISSANT, BUT AUSTRIA IS THE TRUE COUNTRY OF BIRTH FOR THIS FAMOUS PASTRY.

INGREDIENTS

Ingredient	Amount
Active Dry Yeast	1.5 TBSP
Coconut Sugar	1 TBSP
Water	400 ML
Salt	2 TSP
Flour	550 GR
Olive Oil	2 TBSP
Vegan Butter	280 GR
Carob Molasses + Water	1 TBSP + 4 TBSP

DIRECTIONS

STEP I

In a large bowl, whisk active dry yeast, water, oil, sugar, flour and salt together. Mix and knead with your hands for about 10 minutes or until get smooth dough. Cover and chill the dough for at least 1 hour.

STEP II

Transfer dough to a floured surface, make 10 small piece from dough, open each piece wide using a rolling pin. Before putting on top of each other, brush melted vegan butter between each dough piece. Freeze for 15 minutes.

STEP III

When you remove dough from the freezer, open it wide in to a rectangular or round form.
Take remaining vegan butter and spread over the dough. Cut it in to small triangle pieces. Throw a small slit per triangle.

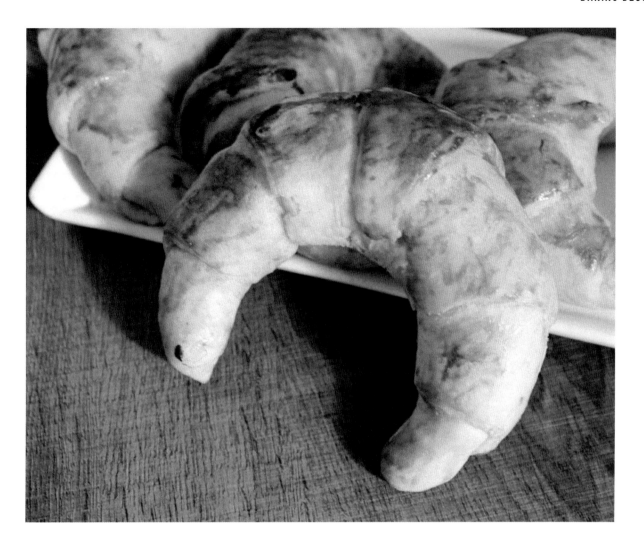

STEP IV
_____

Wrap it and give a croissant shape bending their tails.
Pre-heat oven to 180 degrees.
In a small bowl, mix 1 tbsp carob molasses and 4 tbsp water. Brush over the crois-
sant. Bake them until they are brown color.

Bon Appetit

ALMOND COOKIE

THE WORLD'S EASIEST COOKIES

TIME
20 MINS

SERVING
4

DIFFICULTY
10 / 2

gluten free

INGREDIENTS

Almond Flour	1	CUP
Macadamia Oil	3	TBSP
Confectionery Sugar	3	TBSP
Carob Flour	3	TBSP
Almond Milk	2	TBSP
Vanilla Extract	1	TSP

They are not only soft and a bit chewy - but they're easy to make and are full of flavor.

These light, tender cookies are great served with ice cream as an easy holiday dessert or with simply with a cup of coffee or tea after dinner.

DIRECTIONS

Preheat oven to 175 degrees. In a large bowl, cream together confectionery sugar and macadamia oil. Add all other ingredients and knead with your hands until well blended well. Open dough with a rolling pin. Give a shape with your hands or use a mold. Bake for 8-10 minutes or till cookies are lightly colored

NORDIC
ALMOND COOKIE

PEAR WALNUT CRUMBLE

METHOD
OVEN

TIME
50 MINUTE

SERVING
4-5

BY TRYING THIS RECIPE, GIVE THE CLASSIC APPLE CRUMBLE A MODERN TWIST WITH JUICY PEARS!

INGREDIENTS

Rolled Oats	1+1/2 CUP
Walnut Crushed	1 CUP
Salt	1/2 TSP
Coconut Sugar	7-8 TBSP
Pear	3 MEDIUM
Cinnamon	1 TSP
Cardamom	1 TSP
Vanilla Extract	1 TSP
Lemon Juice	3 TBSP
Cornstarch	1 TSP
Almond Meal	3 TBSP
Coconut Oil	1 TBSP

DIRECTIONS

STEP I

Preheat oven to 180 degrees.
Place a parchment paper into the baking pan.

STEP II

Place pear cubes into the bowl, add 3 tbsp sugar, cinnamon, cardamom, 1/4 tsp salt, vanilla extract, lemon juice and cornstarch, toss together. Cover with foil and bake for about 15 minutes. Set aside.

STEP III

Place 1 cup rolled oats, walnuts, 1/4 tsp salt, vanilla, 2 tbsp coconut sugar and vegan butter into the food processor, mix on high speed. Transfer mixture into the baking pan. Press down into an even layer with your hands. Open foil and spread pear mixture over the crust layer.

STEP IV

Place 2 tablespoon coconut sugar, almond flour, 1/2 cup rolled oats and 1 tablespoon coconut oil into the food processor, mix on high speed and make crumble
with your hands. Top with crumble topping. Place pan into the oven. Bake for 20-
25 minutes or until golden browned. Serve with whipped coconut cream and your
favorite berries or ice cream if desired.

Bon Appetit

VETELÄNGDER
SWEDISH ALMOND BREAD

METHOD
POT

TIME
25 MINUTE

SERVING
4

DOUGH

All purpose flour	400 GR
Lukewarm plant milk	250 GR
Dry active yeast	8 GR
Coconut Sugar	60 GR
Orange Zest	1 LARGE
Salt	1/4 TSP
Vegan Butter	40 GR

FILLING

Almond Flour	1 CUP
Coconut Sugar	1/4 CUP
Coconut Oil	4 TBSP
Cinnamon	1/2 TSP
Cardamom	1/4 TSP
Vanilla Extract	1 TSP
Flaxseed	1 TBSP
Water	3 TBSP

TOPPING

Lupin or Crob Molasses	1 TBSP
Ground Flaxseed + Water	2 TBSP + 6 TBSP
Confectioners Sugar	2 TBSP

DIRECTIONS

STEP I

Mix yeast, lukewarm milk and sugar in a large bowl until yeast is dissolved. Let it rest to activate for 15 minutes. In a small bowl, mix flaxseed and water together. Let it rest in the refrigerator for 15-20 minutes until get sticky.

STEP II

When yeast is activated, then add flour, orange zest, salt mix on low until combined well, then add vegan butter, mix on medium speed for 5-6 minutes or until come together well.
Transfer dough on to the floured surface, knead with your hands for 3-4 minutes. Place dough in a large bowl, cover the bowl with a clean towel. Let it rest in a warm place for 40-45 minutes.

STEP III

When it doubled in size, transfer on to the floured surface, knead for 2-3 minutes. Divide dough into two pieces. Pre-heat oven to 225 degrees. In a large bowl, place all filling ingredients and whisk together on high speed for 4-5 minutes. Using a rolling pin roll the dough 20x25 cm rectangle. Spread almond paste over the dough using a silicon spatula. Roll the dough into a tight log. Cut the log in equal pieces with a knife.

STEP IV
─────────

Repeat the same process for the remaining dough. Place a baking sheet onto the baking pan. Shape the pieces by sticking together right and left. In a small bowl mix egg replacer and water. Brush the tops of the bread with egg replacer. Bake for 15 minutes until golden browned. Let cool at least 20 minutes. Sprinkle with confectioners sugar. Slice and serve!

〰〰〰〰〰〰〰〰〰〰〰〰

Bon Appetit

TOSCATÅRTA
SWEDISH ALMOND CAKE

METHOD
OVEN

TIME
50 MINUTE

SERVING
8

INGREDIENTS

Egg Replacer + water	3 TSP + 90 ML
Coconut Sugar	50 GR
Vanilla Extract	2 TSP
Agave Syrup	4 TBSP
Coconut Oil	50 GR
All Purpose Flour	175 GR
Chestnut Flour	30 GR
Almond Milk	80 ML
Baking Powder	9 GR

TOPPINGS

Vegan Butter	50 GR
Sliced Almonds	80 GR
Maple Syrup	60 GR
Coconut Flour	1 TBSP
Almond Meal	2 TBSP

DIRECTIONS

STEP I

Pre-heat oven to 200 degrees. Lightly oil the spring-form pan, set aside.

STEP II

In a large bowl, whisk coconut sugar, agave, egg replacer and water until fluffy. Add coconut oil and mix well until get a mousse mixture.
Then add all purpose flour, baking powder, vanilla extract and almond milk. Using a mixer, whisk on high speed for 5-6 minutes

STEP III

Pour mixture in a grassed spring-form pan.
Bake at the bottom of the oven for 20-25 minutes or until golden browned. When it is baked, remove from the oven and set aside. Let it cool while making glazing sauce.

STEP IV

To make topping sauce, in a bowl, combine vegan butter, maple and coconut flour until completely smooth. Melt on medium heat for 4-5 minutes. When cake is baked, spread mixture over the cake.
Top with almond flakes and let it cool at least 10 minutes. You can also keep in the refrigerate and serve it cold with a vegan icecream.

Bon Appetit

ICELANDIC VÍNARTERTA

A PERFECT WAY OF ENJOYING WINTER

Vínarterta (Icelandic: Vienna cake), also known as Randalín (striped lady cake), is a multi-layered cake made from alternating layers of almond and figs, cherry or plums. Vinarterta is a classic holiday cake that has become more common in Canada than Iceland.

For best keeping: Put the vinarterta cake box(es) in the refrigerator (or freezer for longer term storage), until ready to cut. If it's frozen, move to refrigeration the night before. Keep refrigerated until ready to cut.

YOUR VINARTERTA CAKE KEEPS WELL FOR 3 WEEKS IN THE RE-
FRIGERATOR AND 3 MONTHS IN THE FREEZER!
BEST WISHES FOR WONDERFUL VINARTERTA EXPERIENCES!

ICELANDIC

VÍNARTERTA

METHOD	TIME	SERVING	DIFFICULTY
OVEN	1 HOUR	6 PERSON	10 / 7

FILLING

1 Cup Water

500 GR Dried Figs

1 Lemon Juice

1 Teaspoon Ground Cardamom

1 Tablespoon Vodka

1 Teaspoon Vanilla Extract

30 GR Coconut Sugar

1/2 Teaspoon Cinnamon

D O U G H

Vegan Butter	150 GR
Confectionery Sugar	40 GR
Egg Replacer + Water	4 TBSP + 100 ML
Flour	100 ML
Ground Cardamom	1/2 TSP
Baking Powder	1 TSP
Vanilla Extract	1 TSP
Almond Milk	2 TBSP

STEP I Place dried figs into the pot, cover with 1 cup water. Bring to boil until boiled down. Place them into the food processor, add filling ingredients; lemon juice, 1 tbsp cardamom, vanilla extract, coconut sugar and cinnamon. Mix on high speed until combined well. Transfer mixture in a bowl. Set aside. Pre-heat oven to 180 degrees.

STEP II In a medium bowl, mix 4 tsp egg replacer and 100 ml. warm water. Add butter, sugar, vanilla extract and mix together until combined well. Place mixture into the food processor, add flour, cardamom and baking powder. Mix on high speed until get dough.

Remove dough from the food processor. Divide into 7 pieces. Roll dough out on to a floured surface using a rolling pin, give a thing and long shape.

Place a baking sheet in a 12 inch cake pan. Place dough in to the pan. Bake for 10 min until soft, but not browned. When the layers are soften, you can easily cut them. When it is baked, let cool it for 5 min at least. Using a knife, spread a layer of the fig mixture over the crust. Place the second crust layer over top. Spread fig mixture again. Repeat the same process for remaining 5 pieces. Slice it. Keep it in a cool and dry place up to 3 days. Decorate with confectionery sugar if desired.

PUDDING

WITH CHOCOLATE AND BERRIES

CHOCOLATE PUDDING

INGREDIENTS

Coconut Sugar	4 TBSP
Raw Cocoa	2 TBSP
Cornstarch GlutenFree	2 TBSP
Cashew Milk	380 ML
Forest Fruits	TO DECORATE
Fresh Mint or Basil	TO DECORATE

METHOD	TIME	SERVING	DIFFICULTY
POT	15 MINUTE	3	10/2

IT REQUIRES ONLY 4 MAIN INGREDIENTS !

Simply Delicious

DIRECTIONS

STEP I

In a medium saucepan, whisk together the coconut sugar, cocoa powder and cornstarch. Slowly pour in the cashew milk and whisk to combine.

STEP II

Cook over medium heat, whisking constantly until the pudding begins to bubble. Cook two minutes longer The mixture will be thick but pourable and will set up more while it chills.

STEP III

Take the saucepan off the heat.
Pour the pudding into the jars and cover.
Refrigerate until well-chilled, 3-4 hours.
Serve with your favorite berries and fresh mint leaves.

Bon Appetit

HALLONGROTTOR

RASPBERRY CAVES

TIME
20 MINS

SERVING
5-6

DIFFICULTY
10 / 5

Chewy

INGREDIENTS

Vegan Butter	175	GR
Whole Wheat Flour	220	GR
Baking Powder	1	TSP
Vanilla Extract	1	TSP
Coconut Sugar	100	GR
Raspberry Jam	1/4	CUP

DIRECTIONS

Pre-heat oven to 200 degrees. In a bowl, mix vegan butter, coconut sugar, vanilla and baking powder together until fluffy. Then add the flour and mix thoroughly with your hands until combined. Place 20 cupcake forms on a baking sheet.

Then divide the dough into 17-18 pieces and roll them into little balls in the cupcake forms and gently press a little hole with your middle of each ball. Place the balls in the cupcake forms and gent with your finger in the middle of each ball. Then place about in each of the holes.
Bake for about 18-20 minutes.

Bon Appetit

HALLONGROTTOR

RASPBERRY CAVES

KLADDKAKA
SWEDISH BROWNIE

METHOD
OVEN

TIME
50 MINUTE

SERVING
8

TOPPINGS

Icing Sugar	TO DECORATE
Coconut Cream	3-4 TBSP
Raspberry	8-9 GR

INGREDIENTS

Egg Replacer (Lupin or Flaxeggs)+ Water	2 TSP + 60 ML
Vegan Butter	100 GR
Coconut Sugar	140 GR
Maple Syrup	40 GR
All Purpose Flour	150 GR
Cacao Powder	4 TBSP
Cashew Milk	1 TBSP
Vanilla Extract	1 TSP
Salt	A PINCH

DIRECTIONS

STEP I

In a large bowl, whisk egg replacer, water, coconut sugar and butter together until fluffy.
Pre-heat oven to 190 degrees.

STEP II

Use a spring-roll pan (20cm), dust it with cacao powder.
Add flour, vanilla and salt into the bowl, mix on high speed until completely smooth mixture.

STEP III

Pour mixture into the pan.
Bake for 20 minutes. Keep on eye on the cake in order to prevent baking too much.
Let it cool at least 1 hour and then cut into slices, sprinkle icing sugar, serve with whipped cream and your favorite berries.

SWEDISH BROWNIE

———————

One of the most popular baked goods to serve is a Swedish kladdkaka. Kladdkaka
is just gooey, chocolate yumminess, kind of like brownies.
Swedish brownies are called "kladdkaka" in Swedish which means stickycake. I
definitely recommend it with oat or coconut cream or ice cream. It isn't as dense
as a regular cake, it is soft and fudgy.

Bon Appetit

GREEN & AWAKE

R A W
D E S S E R T S

HANDMADE SIGNATURE TREATS WITH
THE FINEST INGREDIENTS

Raw desserts often feature a short list
of whole, unprocessed ingredients like
nuts, seeds, and dried fruit. They get their
sweetness from dried fruit, raw agave
nectar, and other natural sweeteners.
No refined or artificial sweeteners here!

4 LAYER

RAW CAKE

CRUST

140 gr. peanut flour,

100 gr. almond flour,

2 tbsp desiccated coconut,

280 gr. medjool dates

2ND LAYER

220 gr. pre-soaked raw cashews,

2 tbsp organic cold press coconut oil,

3 tbsp raw cacao butter melted,

2 tbsp agave syrup,

3 tbsp lemon juice,

2 tsp vanilla extract,

80 gr. banana

THIRD

220 gr. pre-soaked raw cashews,

3 tbsp lingonberry powder (or your favorite berry powder)

2 tbsp agave syrup,

2 tbsp lemon juice,

2 tbsp cold press coconut oil

2 tbsp raw cacao butter melted or irish moss

TOP LAYER

2 ripe avocado

4 tbsp agave syrup

1 tbsp lemon juice

2 tbsp raw cacao butter melted

1 tbsp coconut oil

1 tbsp raw cacao powder

DECORATING

Forest fruits, sliced almonds,

buckini or quinoa pops

DIRECTIONS

1. Place all crust ingredients into the food processor, mix on high speed until completely smooth.Transfer mixture into the spring--form pan (22cm) . Press with your hands, flatten out. Place into the freezer while making 2nd. layer.

2.Place all 2nd layer ingredients into the blender, mix well until completely smooth. Remove pan from the freezer, pour mixture onto the crust layer. Place it into the freezer again at least 45 minutes.

3.Place all third layer into the blender, mix on high speed until completely smooth. Pour mixture over the 2nd layer. Place into the freezer for 2 hours.

4.Place all top layer ingredients into the food processor, mix well until creamy. Using a double boiler, melt mixture very slowly at 42 degrees. Pour mixture onto the third layer. Decorate with berries and sliced almonds or your favorite nuts and berries! Let it rest in the freezer for 3-4 hours before cutting

RAW CAKE

BLUEBERRY AND COCONUT

BLUEBERRY COCONUT CAKE

INGREDIENTS

CRUST

Medjool Dates	170 GR
Almond Meal	150 GR
Coconut Oil	2 TBSP
Salt	1/4 TSP

METHOD
RAW

TIME
3 HOURS

SERVING
8

DIFFICULTY
10/7

WHITE LAYER

Coconut Cream	100 GR
Cashews Pre-soaked	130 GR
Maple or Agave Syrup	2 TBSP
Vanilla Extract	1/2 TSP
Lemon Juice	3 TBSP
Coconut Oil	2 TBSP
Cacao Butter melted	1 TBSP

CHOCOLATE LAYER

Avocado	260 GR
Lemon Juice	2 TBSP
Raw Dark Chocolate	180 GR

DECORATION

Raw Cacao or Shredded Chocolate

Sliced Almonds, Quinoa Pops

1 Cup Fresh Blueberries

Fresh Mint Leaves

DIRECTIONS

STEP I

Place all crust ingredients into the food processor, mix on high speed until get dough.
Line a parchment paper into the spring-form pan (20cm). Transfer mixture into the spring-form pan. Press with your hands, flatten out.

STEP II

Place all white layer ingredients into the blender, mix on high speed until get silky and smooth mixture. Pour mixture onto the crust layer. Flatten out using a spatula. Place it into the freezer while preparing chocolate layer.

STEP III

Using a double boiler, melt chocolate very slowly. Place melted chocolate into the blender, add peeled avocado and lemon juice. Mix on high speed until get silky mixture. our mixture onto the white layer. Sprinkle with shredded chocolate or raw cocoa. Decorate with almond slices, quinoa pops and mint leaves. Let it cool in the refrigerator at least 4 hours before serving!

BROWNIE

RAW

6 - 8   PERSON

INGREDIENTS

BROWNIE ———————

Raw Hazelnuts	55 GR
Raw Walnuts	60 GR
Medjool Dates	130 GRAM
Raw Cacao Powder	20 GRAM
Licorice Salt	A PINCH
Cold Pressed Coconut Oil	1 TBSP
Pure Vanilla Extract	1/2 TSP

FROSTING ———————

Hass Type Avocado	150 GR
Cold Pressed Coconut Oil	1 TBSP
Raw Cacao Powder	25 GR
Licorice Salt	A PINCH
Medjool Dates or Tamarind	60 GR
Cold Press Coffee	1 TBSP
Cinnamon Extract	1/2 TSP

DIRECTIONS

BROWNIE
Combine the brownie ingredients in a food processor and process until a sticky and smooth dough forms.
Transfer to a 15x15 square baking pan (lined with parchment paper or greased with coconut oil).

Press the dough down using a spatula (it's easier if you use your fingers) until flat and firm. Let rest in the fridge while preparing the chocolate and a frosting.

FROSTING
Combine the ingredients for the frosting (except the coconut oil) in the jar of your high speed blender and blend until nice and creamy. Stream the coconut oil into the mixture.

ASSEMBLE
Using an offset spatula spread the frosting evenly over the brownie. Cut into squares and garnish with walnut halves or edible gold. Keep in the refrigerator until ready to eat.

CINNAMON BALLS

R A W

CINNAMON BALLS

METHOD
RAW

TIME
30 MINS

SERVING
8

DIFFICULTY
10/3

INGREDIENTS

Rolled Oats	100 GR
Medjool Dates	125 GR
Cinnamon	1 TSP
Cardamom	1 TSP
Salt	A PINCH
Water	2 TBSP
Cocoa Powder	2 TBSP

These little raw balls are a sure winner over the Christmas period.

They are loaded with cinnamon, which is great for fighting off sugar cravings. Cinnamon increases glucose metabolism which helps regulate our blood sugar levels. It slows the emptying of your stomach to reduce that sugar spike and improves the effectiveness of insulin. Not only this but it also enhances our antioxidant defences!

They have been bound using dates which are a great source of iron, potassium, manganese and calcium!

DIRECTIONS

STEP I

Place oatmeal into the food processor mix on high until powdered. Then add dates and mix on high until sticky.

STEP II

Add 1/2 tsp cinnamon, 1 tbsp cocoa powder and all other ingredients. Mix until completely smooth.

STEP III

In a small bowl, mix remaining cinnamon and cocoa powder, mix. Roll the balls into the cocoa mix. Keep in the refrigerator.

CHOKLADBOLLAR

SWEDISH CHOCOLATE BALLS

TIME
25 MINS

SERVING
35 BALLS

DIFFICULTY
10 / 3

Fika time

INGREDIENTS

Rolled Oats	100 GR
Almond Flour	50 GR
Medjool Dates	130 GR
Carob Flour	2 TBSP
Cacao Powder	2 TBSP
Vanilla Extract	1/2 TSP
Maple or Agave Syrup	2 TSP
Espresso	5 TBSP
Coconut Flakes	4 CUP
Pearl Sugar & Chocolate	TO DECORATE

It requires no cooking, only moulding by hand. And the procedure may be modified according to personal preference: while chocolate balls are typically rolled in pearl sugar, desiccated coconut or sprinkles can also be used. This simplicity, this versatility, make the chokladboll a plausible and effortless dessert on those occasions when you think you have no dessert, but would like some.

DIRECTIONS

Make 1 cup espresso and set aside. Place all ingredients in a food processor and mix on high until you get a smooth dough. Form the balls and roll them into coconut flakes, shredded chocolate or roll them in whatever you desire. Place in the refrigerator for 1 hour before serving! Serve cold!

Bon Appetit

CHOKLADBOLLAR

SWEDISH CHOCOLATE BALLS

MOCHA

RAW CAKE

CRUST

1 cup almond meal
6 medjool dates
1 tbsp raw cacao powder
A pinch of salt
1 tsp pure vanilla powder
1 tbsp coconut oil

FILLING

1 cup pre-soaked raw macadamia
2 tbsp coconut oil
2 tbsp maple syrup
1 shot cold brewed espresso
1 tbsp raw cocoa powder

GLAZING

3 tbsp agave or maple syrup
3 tbsp coconut oil
2 tbsp raw cacao powder
2 tsp vanilla extract
A pinch of salt

TOPPINGS

4 tbsp red currants
raw chocolate nibs

DIRECTIONS

Place all crust ingredients into the food processor, mix on high speed until completely smooth. Then place mixture into the small parfait pans or a medium cake pan. Press it and flatten out with a spatula. Place all filling ingredients into the blender, mix until completely smooth. Pour mixture over the crust. Let it cool at least 2 hours. In a small pan, mix all chocolate topping ingredients well. Pour mixture over the filling layer. Decorate with red currants or berries and raw chocolate nibs or your favorite toppings. Place it into the freezer for about 2 hours. Serve cold!

Bon Appetit

DONUT BALLS

W/ MACADAMIA CREAM

INGREDIENTS

2 cup almond flour

1 cup organic coconut flour

3 tbsp coconut nectar

2 tsp vanilla extract

160 gr. medjool dates

1 lemon juice

4 tbsp coconut oil

MACADAMIA CREAM

100 gr. raw macadamia nuts pre-soaked

3 tbsp coconut cream

25 gr. raw cacao butter melted

2 tbsp lemon juice

3 tbsp agave syrup

1/2 tsp vanilla extract

DECORATING

lingonberry powder

fresh rosemary

DIRECTIONS

Soak dates in warm water for about 15-20 minutes. Then add to the food processor, mix on high for about 2-3 minutes. Add almond flour, coconut flour, syrup, vanilla extract, cardamom, lemon juice and coconut oil into your blender. Mix on high speed until you get dough texture. Remove dough from the blender. Make small balls with your hands. Coat with lingonberry powder. Add soaked, rinsed macadamia nuts into the food processor, add all remaining macadamia cream ingredients, mix on high speed until silky smooth. Aesthetically spread the macadamia cream on the plate. Place balls into the plate carefully. Decorate with fresh rosemary leaves. Keep in the refrigerator at least 2 hours.

Bon Appetit

PUNSCHRULLAR

SWEDISH VACUUM CLEANER

INGREDIENTS

GREEN MARZIPAN

6 tbsp maple syrup

1 small handful of spinach

1/2 tsp spirulina

1 cup almond meal

1/2 cup coconut flour

PUNSCH DOUGH

3 tbsp almond meal

3 tbsp cacao powder

3 tbsp desiccated coconut

12 ripe dates

12 raw cashews

1 tbsp arrack extract

CHOCOLATE SAUCE

150 gr.raw bitter vegan chocolate melted

1 tsp vanilla extract

1 tsp coconut oil

DIRECTIONS

Place all green marzipan dough ingredients in a food processor and mix on high until completely combined. Transfer dough in a large bowl, knead dough with your hands while adding coconut flour until get marzipan texture. Then move it to a oily baking paper, roll the dough flat with using a rolling pin. Blend all punsch dough ingredients into the blender and mix on high for 3-4 minutes. It should be same texture as raw vegan balls. Make long roll of dough with your hands using oily paper. Place punsch dough on top of the green marzipan dough and fold it in. Cut 3 inch rolls and set aside. Melt bitter chocolate and add coconut oil and vanilla extract. Whisk it with a spoon. Then, dip one side of roll. Place in the fridge for 10 minutes. Make the same process another side of punsch rolls. Serve cold!

Bon Appetit

RAW TIRAMISU CAKE

TIRAMISU MEANS "PULL ME UP" IN ITALIAN

Italians believe tiramisu is a strong aphrodisiac, and once you know it's erotic history you'll understand why.

Tiramisu was invented inside brothels in the gorgeous northern Italian town of Treviso, renowned for its sexually relaxed mores and pleasure-seeking inhabitants.

In Italian, tiramisu literally means "pull me up, lift me up", or, more literally, "pull it up".

Italy's iconic dessert as we know it today is made of layers of Savoiardi ladyfingers biscuits dipped one by one in a whipped mixture of mascarpone cream cheese and a fine blend of different coffee powders. Some chefs add Marsala wine and a sprinkle of chocolate powder.

It's a harmony of flavours that triggers ecstasy, and not just in the mouth.

Today there are the hundreds of tiramisu-inspired desserts. Because of the light, fluffy nature of tiramisu, recipes that include fruits and berries are popular spin-offs. Additionally, many recipes attempt to recreate the taste of tiramisu in a slightly different form. Take the "Raw Tiramisu," for example, which has no lady fingers, no mascarpone cheese and no liquor, but instead uses coffee-flavored ice-cream, pound cake and fudge sauce to make a dessert that has the essence of tiramisu. Or, what about the "Tiramisu Pizza," which creates a tiramisu out of sweetened pizza dough with the mascarpone and espresso mix poured on top?

TIRAMISU CAKE

CRUST LAYER

Almond Flour	1/2 CUP
Raw Cashews	85 GR
Coconut Oil	2 TBSP
Medjool Dates	4 LARGE

CHOCOLATE LAYER (OPTIONAL)

Cold Brew Espresso	2 TBSP
Cashew Pre-soaked	95 GR
Raw Chocolate	40 GR
Agave Syrup	2 TBSP
Coconut Oil	1 TBSP
Cashew Milk	3 TBSP

COFFEE MOUSSE LAYER

Raw Cashews	95 GR
Cacao Butter	40 GR
Date Syrup	2 TBSP
Cold Brew Espresso	3 TBSP
Agave Syrup	2 TBSP
Coconut Oil	1 TBSP
Cashew Milk	3 TBSP
Pure Vanilla Extract	1 TSP

CREAM LAYER

Raw Cashews	100 GR
Cacao Butter	40 GR
Agave Syrup	2 TBSP
Coconut Oil	2 TBSP
Coconut Butter	3 TBSP
Cashew Milk	6-7 TBSP

DIRECTIONS

CRUST LAYER

Process all base layer ingredients in your food processor until sticky. Press the mixture into cake tin and place in the freezer to set while you work with your filling.

COFFEE MOUSSE LAYER

In a food processor, process coffee mousse ingredients until smooth. Spread the mixture evenly over the base layer, return to the freezer.

CHOCOLATE LAYER (OPTIONAL)

Once it has hardened. Process chocolate layer until smooth, spread mixture over the coffee mousse layer. (This layer is optional you can add if you prefer to make 4 layer or skip chocolate layer, just add cream layer over the coffee mousse layer.)

CREAM LAYER

Place all ingredients into the blender, rocess cream layer. Set aside 4-5 tbsp cream to decorate using a piping bag later. Then spread cream evenly and freezer to set overnight. Before serving, dust the top with cacao powder, decorate with using star nozzle.

Bon Appetit

RAW SWEDISH PRINCESS CAKE

BASE:

Almond Flour	90	GR
Raisins Paste	100	GR
Coconut Flour	35	GR
Coconut Oil	1	TBSP
Vanilla Extract	1/2	TSP

FILLING:

Raw Cashews soaked	160	GR
Agave Syrup	3	TBSP
Lemon Juice	3	TBSP
Coconut Oil	40	GR
Cacao Butter	25	GR
Coconut Cream	100	GR

MID LAYER:

Raspberry Chia Jam	150	GR
Filling Cream	115	GR
Cacao Butter	15	GR

GREEN MARZIPAN:

Matcha Powder	1/2	TSP
Raw Almond Flour	90	GR
Raw Agave Syrup	4	TBSP
Raw Coconut Flour	20	GR
Bitter Almond Extract	1/4	TSP

TO MAKE THE BASE

To make the base add the almonds and to a food processor and blitz until they are finely ground. Add the remaining ingredients for the base and continue to blitz until all the ingredients are broken down into a crumb. The mixture should press together like a dough between your fingers. Press the dough into the bottom of your cake tin. Pack it down firmly and set aside while you making filling.

FILLING:

To prepare the filling, add the cashews, coconut cream, agave syrup, lemon juice to your blender. Blend until they are smooth. Lastly add in the melted coconut oil, and coconut butter then blend further for 30 seconds to incorporate the oil into the mixture. Take around 100 gr of the cream and set aside to use it in mid layer later.
Pour half of the remaining cream over the cake crust. Place in the freezer to set for 20 minutes to set in order to prevent mixed layers.

TO MAKE MID LAYER:

Make raspberry chia jam according to raw jam recipe in this book. Place in a bowl, add 100 gr of the filling cream and melted cacao butter. Mix well in the bowl. Set aside.

GREEN MARZIPAN:

Place almond and coconut flour into food processor, combine well. Then add agave syrup, almond extract and matcha. Mix until you get sticky dough. If it is too wet, then add more almond flour.

When first cream layer is done, remove from the freeezer, add raspberry layer over the cashew filling, then set in the freezer next 25 minutes. Then pour remaining cashew filling. Freeze for 45 minutes. Remove cake from the mold. Cover with princess layer (green marzipan. Keep in the refrigerator for next 30 minutes before cutting and serve.

a swedish way to enjoy Fika

The name of this dessert "prinsesstårta" which means pricess cake in Swedish. The cake got it's name prinsesstårta because the Swedish princesses loved the cake so much. But what I really wanted to know was what did it have to do with princesses and why was it green? The first recipe was created in the 1930s by Jenny Åkerström. She published a series of four cookbooks called "The Princess Cookbooks" and in one of the editions, there was a recipe for "Grön Tårta" (green cake). A story is that this later became known as "princess cake" (prinsesstårta) because the three princesses are said to have loved it so much. The fourth week in September is known as the week of the "Prinsesstårta!Pronounciation of prinsesstårta: PRIN-sess-TOHR-tah The traditional recipe of this cake consists of spongy layers of cake alternating with jam, vanilla custard and whipped cream topped with a thin layer of bright green marzipan.

PEPPARKAKA THUMBPRINTS

FOR THE DOUGH ————

Sprouted Almond Flour	100 GR
Coconut Flour	2 TBSP
GF Oat Flour	2 TBSP
Gingerbread Spice	1 TSP
Coconut Oil	2 TBSP
Licorice Salt	1 TSP
Coconut Milk	2 TBSP
Coconut Sugar	2 TBSP
Raw Agave Syrup	2 TBSP

DECORATION ————
Raspberry Chia Jam
Tempered Raw Chocolate

DIRECTIONS

1. Start by melting the coconut oil in the double boiler and add the coconut sugar, stirring to dissolve.

2. Add coconut milk and gingerbread spice, stirring so everything mixes.

3. Grind sprouted and dehydrated almonds and oatmeal in a spice grinder to get it ground.

4. Put coconut and oat flour, salt, agave nectar and the rest of the ingredients in a food processor. Process until the dough comes together.

5. Place the dough on a baking sheet paper, cut them about 12 - 14 pieces using a 4cm cutter and roll into a ball. Press the thumb in the middle of the ball.

6. Place a small click of jam in the middle of the balls.

7. Place all cookies on a dehydrator tray and leave in a drying in the dehydrator at 42 ° C for about 2 -3 hours.

8. Melt tempered raw chocolate using a double boiler, transfer to a pipping bag , cut the tip of the pipping bag a bit. Decorate the corners of cookies by pouring thin 3-4 lines from chocolate. Let it cool for a hour in the fridge before serving.

Storage: Keep in the refrigerator up to a week, in the freezer up to 3 months.

PEPPARKAKA THUBPRINTS

R A W

BLUEBERRY
NICE CREAM

METHOD
RAW

TIME
10 MINUTE

SERVING
2

TOPPINGS

1 Slice coconut meat cut
into star pieces,

1 tbsp Amaranth pops

1 Passion fruit

A handful of Raspberries

INGREDIENTS

Frozen Blueberry	100	GR
Maca Powder	2	TSP
Hemp Protein	2	TSP
Frozen Banana	3	RIPE
Peanut Butter	2	TBSP
Coconut Milk	4	TBSP

DIRECTIONS

Place blueberries, maca powder, hemp protein, banana, peanut butter and coconut milk into the blender, mixon high speed.
Using small star cutter, cut fresh coconut meat into star pieces. Top on smoothie.
Sprinkle amaranth pops.
Add passion fruit and blueberries. Serve cold!

Notes: Substitute peanut butter with almond, walnut, hazelnut or sunflower seed butters for variety of flavors.

Bon Appetit

———————————

The secret about nice cream is in the bananas. There is some magic that happens when bananas are frozen.

They become the perfect smooth and creamy base for ice cream with endless possibilities to experiment with. When ripe bananas are frozen they act like a binding agent for our nice cream so you don't need any milk but if you need a liquid consistency, just add a little plant milk.

Another fun part of this recipe are the toppings. Lots of possibilities here, as well. Try sliced fruit, seeds and nuts, coconut flakes, cacao nibs and all kinds of powders and spices. Make your favorite version and let the people around you guess what's in it.

OATMEAL
RAW & COOKED-TWO WAYS

METHOD
RAW

TIME
15 MINUTE

SERVING
2

TOPPINGS

Buckini (activated & dehydrated buckwheats)

Sliced strawberries and blueberries

or whatever you like.

INGREDIENTS

1 cup rolled oats

1.5 -2 cups water or almond milk

1 tbsp raw agave or more if you need

(alternatively dates can be added)

1/4 tsp pink himalayan salt

1/2 tsp cinnamon extract or powder

DIRECTIONS

1. Soak the oats for at least a couple of hours minimum, but better to soak them overnight in 4 cups of water if you have the time. In the morning strain and add 2 cups of clear water or plant based milk.

2. If you're using dates in the place of agave , you may want to soak the dates as well, you can use the date soak water as part, or all, of the 2 cups needed in the recipe to make it just a little bit sweeter.

3. Next ,place the rinsed oats, dates, and the two cups of water (or, use some of the date soak water) in a blender or food processor and blend or process on high speed for about 25 seconds or until the mixture is smooth.

4. To make RAW, place into a bowl and cover. Move to food dehydrator. Cook at 42 C for 2-3 hours or until soften and warm enough. Mix well. Taste it, add more cinnamon or sweetener if you need.
To cooked version, transfer mixture in a pot, on low-medium heat stir well until soften enough. Once cooked, divide between bowls.

5. Top with chopped blueberries, strawberries, cinnamon powder and buckinis. Drizzle extra maple or agave syrup if desired.

Bon Appetit

OATMEAL

RAW & COOKED - 2 WAYS

ACAI BOWL

METHOD
RAW

TIME
5 MINUTES

SERVING
2

TOPPINGS

Pumpkin seeds, sunflower seeds,
freeze dried raspberries, fresh
sage leaves, coconut chips,
chopped hazelnuts

INGREDIENTS

Ingredient	Amount
Ripe Frozen Banana	4
Frozen Mixed Berries	1 CUP
Baby Spinach	A HANDFULL
Tahini (or peanutbutter)	1 TBSP
Maca Powder	1 TSP
Acai Powder	1 TBSP

DIRECTIONS

1. Place all the ingredients expect decoration ingredients in blender and blend until completely smooth. We want it thick and smooth, so avoid adding liquid.

2. Pour in a bowl, top with desired toppings.

3. Eat cold!

Bon Appetit

BANANA RASPBERRY SPICE SMOOTHIE

METHOD
RAW

TIME
10 MINUTE

SERVING
2

INGREDIENTS

Ripe Banana	2
Raspberry	1 CUP
Coconut Milk	1 CUP
Cinnamon	1/8 TSP
Cardamom	1/8 TSP
Nutmeg	1/8 TSP

TOPPINGS

Raspberry

Fresh Basil Leaves

Quinoa Pops

DIRECTIONS

Place banana, raspberry and coconut milk into the blender.
Mix on high speed until smooth. Add spice mix and stir well.
Pour mixture into glasses.
Decorate with fresh raspberry, basil leaves and quinoa pops if desired.

Bon Appetit

SPINACH BANANA SMOOTHIE

METHOD
RAW

TIME
10 MINUTE

SERVING
2

TOPPINGS

Star Flower (borage)

Sliced Almonds

INGREDIENTS

Ripe Banana	2
Frozen Spinach	1 CUP
Almond Milk	1 CUP
Spirulina	1 TSP
Peanut Butter	1 TBSP
Fresh Sukkari Dates	3-4
Nutmeg	A PINCH

DIRECTIONS

1. Place banana, spinach , dates, peanut butter, and almond milk into the blender.

2. Mix on high speed until smooth. Add nutmeg and stir well.

3. Pour mixture into glasses.

4. Decorate with sliced almonds and star flower if desired. Enjoy cold!

Bon Appetit

RAW
OREO

METHOD
RAW

TIME
30 MINUTE

SERVING
5-6

COOKIE

1/2 cup oat flour,

1/2 cup coconut flour

2 tbsp cacao powder,

6-8 large medjool dates pitted,

soaked in hot water,

1 tbsp melted coconut oil

FILLING

1/2 cup raw cashews soaked

in water for 6 hours,

1 tbsp cacao butter melted,

2 tbsp lemon juice,

1 tbsp maple or agave syrup,

1/2 tsp vanilla extract

DIRECTIONS

1. Place all dough ingredients into food processor and mix until it reaches a dough-like consistency.

2. Line a flat surface or large cutting board with parchment paper and place the dough in the center. Use a rolling pin to roll the dough into an even, roughly 1/4-inch-thick rectangle. Cut in circle shapes with cookie cutter.

3. Place filling ingredients into the food processor, mix on high speed until you get paste form. Top half of the cookies with roughly 1 tsp filling cream.

4. Put in the freezer to chill for just a few minutes. Then put another circle top on the cookie.

5. Refrigerate at least 2 hours before consuming.
They tend to soften when at room temperature so keep them in the fridge.
You can also keep them in the freezer up to 1 month.

Bon Appetit

RAW LOG CAKE

8-10 PERSON

DOUGH:

Raw Almond Flour	170	GR
Raw Oat Flour	50	GR
Medjool Dates	100	GR
Raw Cacao Powder	4	TBSP
Raw Agave Syrup	2	TBSP
Vanilla Powder	1	TSP
Coconut Milk	3	TBSP
Licorice Salt	1/2	TSP

VANILLA CREAM:

Raw Cashews soaked	150	GR
Coconut Cream	3	TBSP
Lemon Juice	1+ 1/2	TBSP
Agave Syrup	2	TBSP
Coconut Oil	1	TBSP
Cacao Butter	2	TBSP
Vanilla Extract	1	TSP

TO MAKE THE BASE

Start by making the dough. To do this add the oats to a food processor and blend until a flour forms. Then add the ground almonds and cacao powder - blend again to fully combine together.

Pit the dates and add them to the food processor as well as the agave syrup, vanilla, coconut milk and licorice salt. Blend until a thick, sticky mixture forms. Lay out a piece of parchment paper on your kitchen surface and place the chocolate sponge mixture in the centre of it.

Cover with another sheet of parchment paper and roll into a rectangular shape. Remove the paper and neaten up the edges of the rectangle.

FILLING:

To make cream, drain and rinse your soaked cashews and add them to a food processor along with all the other vanilla cream ingredients. Blend until smooth and creamy. Transfer in a bowl, let it cool in the freezer for 15-20 minutes. When it is paste-like consistency, then remove.

ASSEMBLE:

Spread the vanilla cream over the rolled out sponge evenly. Slowly roll the roulade up tightly, using the parchment paper that's underneath the roulade to help with this. Carefully place the roulade into the freezer. Allow to chill where it'll set for at least 30 minutes. Remove from the freezer 10 minutes before cutting and serving! If you want to cover cake with chocolate follow next step on the right page.

CHOCOLATE COVER

Bitter Vegan Chocolate	200	GR
Hass Type Avocado	1	LARGE
Lemon Juice	1	TBSP
Coconut Cream	2-3	TBSP
Coconut Oil	1	TBSP

1. Using a double boiler, melt the chocolate. Transfer into a food processor.

2. Add peeled chopped avocado, lemon juice, coconut cream and coconut oil to fooc processor.

3. Mix on high speed until silky smooth.

4. Pour mixture over the cake when the cake is frozen. This will make process simple.

5. With a fork, create some texture and grooves like the bark on the tree. Dust some powdered sugar if desired or grated chocolate.

6. Freeze for a hour. Decorate with berries , cut and serve.

keyword INDEX

A

B

C

E

F

Q

R

S

T

V

Z

NOTES

GREEN AND AWAKE

NOTES

GREEN AND AWAKE

_____

_____

_____

_____

_____

_____

_____

_____

_____

_____

_____

_____

_____

_____

_____

_____

_____

GREEN & AWAKE

NOTES

GREEN AND AWAKE

_____

GREEN & AWAKE

NOTES

GREEN AND AWAKE

NOTES

GREEN AND AWAKE

NOTES

GREEN AND AWAKE

GREEN & AWAKE

214

This book is the second edition of my first book.

If you like this book and want to see more recipes like these, you may be interested in my other books. Please check my other cookbooks on **gurmevegan.com** or **amazon.com**

Nazli Denli

Manufactured by Amazon.ca
Bolton, ON